All information provided is for educational purposes only.

Ninette Denise Uzan-Nemitz is not an investment adviser and is not recommending any investments. All trades and techniques mentioned in this work are exclusively from her own experience.

Investing in financial markets and day-trading may be risky, potentially resulting in loss of money.

Some names have been changed to respect their privacy.

REMINISCENCES
OF A WALL STREET
TRADER

Ninette Denise UZAN-NEMITZ

For my sons, Thierry and Max, who have made it all worthwhile. Max, by choosing a career in finance, you have honored me more than you know. With all my heart, I hope these words will inspire you both to keep striving for personal and professional excellence.

Contents

When we want, we can.

Trader

Tools & Analyses

When we want, we can.

PREFACE

To live is to be musical, starting with the blood dancing in your veins.
Everything living has a rhythm. Do you feel your music?

—*Michael Jackson*

There is a heartbeat in the world markets.

These cycles, rhythms and contractions seem totally chaotic to the casual observer and the novice investor, while perfectly understood by professional traders. As for the rhythms and cycles of my life, they changed forever when I was still very young and I felt the heartbeat and contractions of my first child.

Children increase our awareness of potential dangers, force us to think, to plan for the future, and often we find ourselves doing much more for their well-being than we would do for ourselves.

This story, my story, shows how a young, naive French girl came to America, learned to manage the markets, found the strength to compete with the men who stood in her way, and sometimes even beat them, out of the need to support her children.

The following pages detail the trials and tribulations of trading. You will find not only the pitfalls to avoid, but the basic principles for success. You will learn about the indicators that the pros use to define and refine their most effective strategies.

And I hope that you will also find the expertise to manage the risks of trading, as well as those of your life.

With diligence and discipline, over time erratic market movements will become rhythmic pulses that will help you feel the market's mood, while anticipating the kicks and sensing the rhythm of its breath.

Most aspiring traders fail and give up quickly. It could have happened to me—it almost did. I wanted to make as much money as possible, as quickly as possible. But I soon realized that concentrating on improving my attitude rather than my profits gave me the greatest return.

For over twenty years, I have been obsessed with the market. It is an unforgiving teacher, even for the most diligent student. I was lucky in having the chance to learn the business with one of the top hedge fund managers… And now I invite you to the reminiscences of a Wall Street trader.

INTRODUCTION

*The man who goes farthest is generally the one who is willing
to do and dare. The sure-thing boat never gets far from shore.*

—*Dale Carnegie*

Staring at one of the five screens of my trading platform, I
followed the price of an ounce of gold carefully. It appeared to be
stabilizing around $257. I called the COMEX broker, working my
order, and smiled into the phone.

"Excellent job! Continue quietly to buy small batches of twenty
to thirty contracts without moving the market. When you get to a
ton of physical gold, call me."

I just had to wait.

Outside, the weather was beautiful. Rockefeller Center was full
of flowers and the sun shone off the leaves of the shrubs. Summer
had always been my favorite time of year and in July 1999, I was
particularly pleased to be living in New York City.

For just a moment, my thoughts shifted away from the streaming
quotes.

I saw myself years earlier, abandoned and hopeless, lost among
the shadows of the towering skyscrapers of Manhattan. The city
never sleeps. Its endless energy seems to come from draining the
souls of its citizens, as greedily as downing the first cup of joe.

My tears of despair had dried and turned into tenacity. I had
managed to cultivate a talent for trading. Now, I was free and
independent. My only opponent was the market, and I knew how to
negotiate with it.

Although a 'typical' trader was an educated, headstrong, and shrewd man dressed as sharp as his personality, I lacked those required credentials. Being foreign, female, and not fresh out of a top MBA program all counted against me.

Still $257… good. I smiled and stood up to stretch my legs.

During my childhood and the first years of my marriage in Paris, I had never asked about opportunities leading to profitable investments, the operation of stock exchanges, or the choice of products traded in the financial world. I knew nothing of financial matters, or of the interest and fascination they held. After my early marriage, I had simply accepted my husband's choice of financial products, which turned out to be a deck of playing cards.

It would have been impossible to imagine in those days that I would be driven to an unknown world and that an extraordinary adventure was going to test my cool and put my mettle to the test.

Unbelievable yet true. Despite my background, I became a portfolio manager and trader, betting very large sums.

Traders have a reputation for being great gamblers but, oddly, I had always been indifferent to gambling. Lottery fever was unknown to me and I did not have the slightest interest in betting.

My only memory of a casino was of an occasion when I accompanied my husband. I was denied entry to the table games since I was a minor, even if a visibly pregnant one. Instead I spent the entire evening sitting in the hall, happily reading my book, which seemed more profitable than the slot machines.

But then, through a series of painful and unpredictable events, I found myself on a different path.

This path led me into the middle of the world's biggest money games, which the bulls, bears and wolves played on Wall Street. Challenge after challenge forced me to find essential character traits that I had never known I possessed.

How strange that now I had the opportunity, the courage, and the capital to bet in the world's biggest casino.

Back in front of the flickering screen, I looked at the picture of my sons on my desk and sighed. I still had a lot of work to do as both their mother and father. But I knew I had what it took. Long ago I had found that the source of my strength came from a desperate desire to provide for them a safe place to live and the opportunity to learn.

What began as a struggle to survive and to provide for my two little boys had turned into a daily battle with my own ignorance and against men's arrogance. A life of which I could not even have dreamt had slowly emerged as my persistence transformed into passion.

FROM PARIS TO NEW YORK

The difference between the impossible and the possible lies in a man's determination.

—*Tommy Lagord*

At fifteen, I was an early bloomer. My body matured faster than my mind and I had the look of a woman. My wish for independence had developed with my body, but my Parisian parents were eager to protect my sister and myself, and forbade us to go out unaccompanied by a chaperone, while our brothers were much freer.

At my sister's engagement party, I had the sudden revelation that it was enough to be married to be autonomous. If I could marry, life would be romantic and exciting. I would be considered an adult and no longer a little girl.

Of course, we would live happily ever after.

One of the guests at the engagement party was introduced to me. He worked in the music business, like my future brother-in-law, and he complimented me on my pretty voice. It was the first time that a man had shown any interest in me and I was flattered and excited by the attentions of this older man. Resolutely, I decided he would be my husband.

A few months later, I managed to convince my parents that this was not the whimsical demand of a spoiled child. They tried to reason with me, but naturally this determined sixteen-year-old thought she knew better. Despite my parents' obvious reluctance, and the clear disapproval of my future husband's family, we were married.

Obviously, the dream of life dancing lovingly in the moonlight, night after night, had been unrealistic. I was far too young and immature and my husband already had his own set of friends and his own interests. We had almost nothing in common, as we soon discovered.

In an attempt to hold the marriage together I had a baby and then a second one, but my hopes of a family strengthening our relationship were doomed to disappointment.

The marriage ended in an early divorce, and the shock and sense of rejection affected my health. I became so sick and emaciated that I ended up in hospital. As a result my ex-husband gained custody of our children, and this depressed me even more. Only the thought of my two lovely little boys gave me any desire to live.

Youth, however, has remarkable powers of recuperation.

I have often been asked what brought me to America. I cannot pretend that it was ambition, or a desire to have a profession and become a leading female icon, although that is what happened. No, my reason for leaving France and going to America was simple. I fell in love.

When I was discharged from the hospital and on the road to recovery, I went to visit friends in Spain and, on a golf course, I met a tall, handsome man who looked like a statue.

Karl was 24 years old, much the same age as me, and he was an American supermodel. During a break from shooting a sportswear advertisement, he noticed that I was practicing my swing and had come to help me correct my position. Thereupon he invited me to join the whole crew, for a refreshing drink. Since school, I had always liked speaking English and our conversation was delightful on all the subjects that we discussed that day.

The next afternoon, as soon as he was free, he invited me to the beach. Upon our arrival, so that my feet would not touch the hot sand of Marbella, he raised me like I was a feather. I was surprised that such a force was manifested with such sweet tenderness and, in an instant, this embrace came as a thunderbolt of passion, both for me and for him.

In a few days, all my hopes for love were answered and even exceeded. Finally, I discovered the languorous romantic evenings and dancing under the starry sky.

We were very young, we were in love, and some time later, we were married and I followed him to live in New York.

Shortly afterwards my ex-husband and I agreed that I should take care of our children and, to my great joy, they came to live with me in America.

However, although Karl enjoyed playing ball with my two little boys and was fond of them, it soon became clear that he felt trapped by the burden of helping to raise two children who were not his. This was clearly more than he had bargained for and I was asked to choose between my new husband and my children.

I was torn by his decision but I gave priority to the welfare of my boys and I left him, bitterly disillusioned and bruised to see our great happiness destroyed so easily.

Thus, shortly after leaving Paris for America, I was divorced again.

My heart was broken and so were my dreams, once more. I felt not only abandoned but terribly hurt, although I hid my tears not to worry my children.

Over time, the immense joy of having my sons with me would heal my wounds. The problem was that I did not have official custody, only a letter from their father allowing me to raise them and therefore, I didn't receive any financial support.

I was young and inexperienced, without resources or alimony and I was too proud to ask for help from anyone. Urgently, I had to find how I would assume this responsibility alone. Time to really grow up.

There was no question of returning to France to rely on my parents. I preferred them to know nothing about my problems. I had to act like an adult, have the courage to live up to this terrible situation and survive the bad times.

Three years earlier, I had written a song that had got a little success in France and on that occasion, I had met people from show business in the United States, whose business cards I had kept.

Not knowing anyone else, I contacted one of these people to ask for a job and I was lucky enough to be hired by a record producer, whose offices were on Broadway. My salary was small but it was better than nothing, even if I still had trouble raising my children decently.

The only solution was to find extra work to earn a bit more and that, as soon as possible.

I had the idea of enrolling at NYU (New York University) in night classes to get a real estate license. With this qualification, I could work on weekends to sell or rent apartments. If a transaction was concluded, the seller paid a commission to the agent. This represented 6% of the price received for the house and was paid to my employer the day of the transaction. For rentals, the percentage was 15% based on the total rent for the year and, of these commissions, I was paid half.

Selling a large apartment could double my salary, so that was promising, but my efforts mainly resulted in rentals. Regardless, while working seven days a week, I managed to meet our needs more easily.

I had visited public schools and found some of them dangerous. The vulgarity of the students in the yard and the metal detectors at each door, to prevent children from carrying guns, had really alarmed me. This second job allowed me to enroll my sons at the French School of New York. The tuition in this excellent institution cost almost as much as my salary and I relied on my second job in order to pay the rent and to buy food ... Indeed, I was facing tremendous pressure.

Every morning, I consulted the New York Times ads to find the latest offers.

Also, I explored the obituaries to do a little investigation and find out whether the family wanted to get rid of the deceased's property. If the estate was to be divided among the heirs, I hoped to have a chance to propose a buyer.

One day, while flipping through the pages randomly, my eyes fell on a proposal to become a broker. It promised to pay one hundred thousand dollars a year, without specifying further details.

Obviously, I probably did not have the qualifications for this position, but I tried to imagine what was required and, upon reflection, I decided to contact this company for more information. I hoped to learn something or at least receive some clues that might be helpful. I had nothing to lose and, basically, I was convinced that trying nothing would bring nothing.

Out of curiosity, I called the number listed and to my surprise, I was invited to come in the next day for an interview in the heart of Wall Street.

WALL STREET

*Wall Street is the only place that people ride to in a
Rolls Royce to get advice from those who take the subway.*

— *Warren Buffet*

Hamilton-Grant was a firm specializing in "penny-stocks" (securities worth a few cents).

I really had no idea what to expect, but as always I had dressed in an elegant suit and was wearing high heels. If I really had the opportunity here to earn enough money to support us in some comfort, I was determined to give myself every chance. I hoped that my serious, professional appearance made it clear that I meant business!

A very big man with graying hair and beard welcomed me into Hamilton-Grant with a large smile. He appeared to wait for me to speak so I asked him for details of what was required. He explained that the job consisted of selling stocks over the phone to anyone who could pay for them.

This gave me some confidence as I had experience, from my real estate work, of being charming to potential buyers on the phone. My spoken English was already close to excellent and I hoped that my French accent was not a disadvantage.

To my surprise I was asked no questions at all about my education or knowledge of financial matters. Instead, while we chatted of everyday matters such as rental prices in New York, this big man's piercing eyes were looking at me as if trying to decide if my fit appearance and young face meant I was a dumb blond...

Obviously, he made up his mind to the contrary and, although it must have been reasonably clear that I had no real background in finance, the manager offered me a job after this fairly short conversation and asked me to start immediately. He assured me that I would receive a 'draw' on future commissions (a payment in advance) and told me that he would pay for the cost of education to acquire my broker's license.

Why me?

This question burned on my lips, but I had enough sense not to ask it. Yet, he knew he owed me an explanation and, with a smile, he said that pretty singles girls were generally excellent brokers. Apparently, he was not worried.

I promised to stay for six months after obtaining the license.

At the end of an accelerated training, exams were held on a Saturday. Very early on the morning of October 17, I went to a school where every classroom would receive many candidates.

We were probably several hundred taking the test that day.

Despite a long examination lasting the whole day, with 250 questions in the morning and 250 in the afternoon, I was not too worried. For important things, I had a certain ease in keeping my composure. Naturally, I had studied a lot and I was going to do my best. My habit always to sit in the front row during my classes, to better absorb the words of the teacher, had greatly facilitated my understanding and I felt ready.

If I failed my chances in the firm were lost, but there was no question I would have any negative thoughts.

Everything with math was simple enough. What I found difficult was that many of the questions included two, sometimes three negations. I had to read them several times before understanding what was asked of me, especially as my knowledge of the language was not perfect. I applied myself so as not to make any mistakes.

At the time, the number of people admitted was less than 50 percent of the competitors. However, although English was not my native language, I passed and the license was sent to Hamilton-Grant.

Amazingly, I was now a licensed broker!

But the following Monday was October 19, 1987, the day of the stock market crash in New York.

All the newspapers featured it and everyone panicked. As for me, I detached myself from the fright of the moment and I remained pragmatic as I knew I would have a real problem getting started in my new job, whether there had been a stock market crash or not.

My challenge was to sell securities that were not traded on a stock exchange and whose values were only available on the "Pink Sheets" (a printed price information of quotes, listing companies which were not required to meet certain minimum regulatory requirements).

These investments were reputed to be riskier and, therefore, the time of my entry into the career of broker could hardly have been worse.

The company I was working for was "Market-Maker" of about twenty of these risky stocks. Half the fee charged to the customer returned to the broker. This "Payout" was 14% higher than the usual compensation of about 36%. It was generous, although the difference was not too far from normal.

But while commissions on listed shares were virtually insignificant, those received on securities issued by the brokerage firm were, in comparison, paid royally. The detail of their calculation was incredible.

How?

If the bid (price at which there was a buyer and therefore where you could sell) was quoted fifty cents and the offer (supply and price at which you could buy) at one dollar, the difference (or spread) of fifty cents was the commission, shared between the firm and the broker. So the customer paid 50% of the purchase price as a premium.

For example, the purchase for fifty thousand dollars of IBM stock at $100, was about 500 shares on which the client added $300 commission, representing 0.6% of the price. However, if I took an order for the same amount on a stock for which Hamilton-Grant made the market, listed at $0.50 - $1.00, no commission was added, but the difference of twenty five thousand dollars (or fifty percent) went to my firm and twelve thousand five hundred dollars were paid to me.

The catch, from the buyer's point of view, was that if he wanted to sell the investment he had acquired for fifty thousand dollars, and the price remained the same, he could not recover more than twenty five thousand dollars, as the value of its acquisition represented only half of the money he had paid.

And it was legal!

Of course, Hamilton-Grant preferred us to work with these in-house securities. For several weeks, I called the phone numbers out of a list of potential customers, but most did not even take the time to listen. They hung up when they heard my French accent or when I announced who I was working for.

As for the ones who did not immediately hang up, there were few who intended to invest. I made a few sales but I was far from covering the amount of my monthly advance ... My debt to my boss increased rapidly and I doubted that I could open enough accounts to cover my draw.

My second job in real estate did not represent a regular income and I began to worry more and more each day.

As time passed, fear seized me. It seemed quite impossible that I would ever be able to produce enough sales to cover my advance.

Posing for Playboy

It is not enough to have a good mind. The main thing is to use it well.

—*René Descartes*

One morning, my boss called me into his office to show me a classified ad that read:

-Every young woman working on Wall Street is invited to a casting for models-

Incredulous, I looked up from the newspaper clipping with a raised eyebrow.

"If you're chosen, your success is assured!" He told me emphatically.

"What!" I exclaimed in shock. "How can Playboy have anything to do with working as a broker?"

Yes, the ad was from Playboy magazine and I was surprised and offended by the suggestion that I would be interested. There was no way I would agree.

"Come on, think!" my boss said stubbornly. "By agreeing to talk to them, you don't risk anything ... they're not looking for nude models; they're just fascinated by women in a men's world. You'll get your name, and ours, known. I've already contacted the reporter and he'll call you this afternoon."

Irritated, I was unable to answer. With a look of annoyance, I nodded my head and returned to my office, worried that he could detect my fears of not being able to cover the salary that was paid to me. I wondered if I gave the impression of being desperate and my pride was tinged.

Yet, I persuaded myself that the Playboy "invitation" was just to be an innocent conversation for a well-known publication and that I should be honored rather than offended. I planned what I might say about working as a broker.

A few hours later, I answered a call from the Playboy reporter.

"Hello, I hope you don't mind my calling you. I work for Playboy Enterprises and I'm writing an article about women on Wall Street. May I take a few minutes of your time?"

His voice was warm and friendly.

"Yes, of course." I tried to sound confident and important.

"What are your comments on the fact that your business is traditionally reserved for men? Is it difficult to compete at their level?"

Knowing he would ask, I had prepared this answer in advance, "This profession is a bit like swimming with sharks, only the strongest survive. However success isn't achieved by force but by intelligence. Many women try to be one of the boys, although I'm still feminine because it's the performance of the financial bottom line that counts and not your appearance, style or behavior. Everyone has their own way of doing things, but only the best will win."

I spoke with assurance and aplomb, trying to give the impression of being an established broker. I did not want him to know that I was new in my profession and that I was having a lot of trouble keeping afloat.

During the interview, all his questions focused on the difficulties of being a woman in a male-dominated business. Then, one of them was more personal:

"What are your dreams?"

"Working in Mergers & Acquisitions, and then to find my Prince Charming and merge with him."

"I really appreciate the relevance and insight of your answers. This is just the kind of material we are looking for. I wonder if you would be willing to come down to the Playboy offices on Third Avenue to talk a bit more?"

Although very surprised by his invitation, I forgot my initial resistance and agreed to a further interview three days later.

I was received at Playboy with respect. The reporter gave me some details of the upcoming featured article.

"We're having a special edition entitled "Women of Wall Street"and we've already had over 900 women applying to appear."

"Well, there aren't 900 women on Wall Street," I exclaimed.

"Oh, I think if you add all the typists and cleaners," he said, and we laughed together.

He continued, "Of course it's normal for the stars featuring in our articles to undress before being photographed, but…

He could see my shocked expression and imminent refusal and added quickly, "if you were chosen, any photograph would be as decent as you wanted."

I was not convinced, but I agreed to leave my address and to have a photograph taken of my face "to help with the selection."

Courteous to the end, the reporter showed me to the door and, as I was leaving he said nonchalantly, "I forgot to mention the fee that is paid to whoever is selected by the editor," and he mentioned a sum that almost took my breath away.

Instinctively, I imagined what this money could buy my children … but I managed not to show anything.

Sometime later, and to my surprise, I was chosen.

Although my first reaction, in spite of the promised fee, was categorically to reject the idea, I felt influenced by my manager who assured me that the publicity could be a good thing for his company and for me. He told me that I would not have to seek customers afterward and instead, they would come to me themselves, happy to have a pretty girl for a broker.

Of course, with significant expenditures for my kids' education, the prospect of not having to worry about the lack of money to raise my boys properly was quite reassuring.

But frankly, another reason made me change my mind. I hoped this pictorial venture would help me regain my confidence and heal the deep pain I always felt, since my break up with Karl and the way in which the children's father had abandoned us. I had no contact with him and he did not call once to inquire about the children.

With the prospect of a better life for my sons in New York, I agreed to pose for Playboy on the condition that I kept on my panties and showed only what girls expose on the beaches of Saint-Tropez.

Now that I finally had the opportunity of developing my sales, I decided to take my work in hand and, instead of calling names on a list in the dark to try to open accounts, I used all my time in the office to analyze the stocks of my employer.

I studied each company in more detail in order to select one that would be more "marketable." My goal was to find a particular product or service whose potential would be easily accepted and would be of interest to buyers.

One caught my attention, a remedy to treat impotence that had been discovered by an unknown biological research company, part of the securities on which I had to work. Looking for what I could find on the subject, I spotted a study conducted in Boston, concluding that 52% of men between 40 and 70 years had this problem in the United States.

With this information, I decided to base my "sales pitch" on the fact that this invention would revolutionize the pharmaceutical industry.

At that time, nobody had heard of this drug and the blue pill did not exist...

A few days later, I met the group of the editorial project for Playboy to arrange the dates and different locations chosen for the filming, including the New York Stock Exchange.

From the first day of shooting, the entire team of the magazine was pleasantly attentive while remaining extremely professional. Everyone was relentlessly busy checking the details of makeup, lingerie or lighting and each crew member respected me as if I was a great personality.

In the early sessions, I was a little tense about being the center of attention, but the photographer reassured me with kind words and encouragement. He was a charming and affable man, who obviously had a lot of experience in working with models who initially felt shy and nervous.

As a result, after a few minutes I forgot the flurry of camera clicks and felt almost as comfortable as if I had been alone.

I was only hoping that my father would never find out!

From a Studio to a 2br

The only true wisdom is knowing that you know nothing.

—*Socrates*

My idea of working on the shares of the company that discovered the cure for impotency was well received. My selling points were excellent. Very soon, I was getting great results and wrote regular tickets of ten thousand shares on a price listed at one dollar per share.

I earned a lot of money quickly and after only three months, the tiny studio where I had to shut the folding table to open the children's beds, was swapped for an apartment in the same building, with two bedrooms and a large living room.

It was a real luxury!

However, at the office, a detail would soon darken the result of my activities. If I could sell those shares in large number, I did not have the right to accept that a client sell his shares to take profits and, if really stressed, I had to find another buyer for the same amount, establishing a "cross-trade" (surrender shares from a seller to a new buyer without affecting the market) to avoid lowering the price.

To make matters worse, a much more serious problem was revealed to me. While my sales grew successfully, I was informed that the drug was administered by being injected into the patient's penis! Despite my research, I had known nothing of this before and I imagined with horror that some individuals might be tempted to stick a syringe into this delicate area with dire results...and dire publicity!

It was imperative to get all my clients out of this investment as soon as possible and I had to work out a strategy for doing this.

Fortunately, the six months that I had agreed to work for Hamilton-Grant were coming to an end and I set out to find the best opportunities for continuing my career.

I applied to Paine Webber, a prestigious firm. After a job interview, I received a generous employment offer, with the agreement that I could start as soon as I was free.

This change gave me the hope of not disappointing my clients, who had hitherto been very pleased with the pharmaceutical investment, whose value rose a little each day. With relief, I would be able to leave the penny-stocks and transfer my "book" (portfolio) to a renowned brokerage house where my clients would be able to sell their shares without problem and benefit from higher quality services.

As soon as the six month commitment was up, I resigned, to the disappointment of my manager and, to enjoy a little vacation before I moved into my new position, I took the kids to Disney World for two weeks. This trip was a well-deserved rest; our stay and all the entertainment were delightful.

I was relaxed for the first time in many months and finally, my life seemed softer. I was no longer afraid and I had found a reason to have confidence in the future.

Meanwhile, in Hamilton-Grant, all the brokers had begun working on the shares of that drug company and, thanks to the increased interest, its price multiplied.

This magnified value attracted the greed of new investors and, as it snowballed, purchases inflated the price even more.

It was a godsend.

Back in New York, on the first day at my new employer, I called all those who had bought the stock on my recommendation and advised them to take their profits immediately, allowing me to transfer their account. They agreed and despite my sales, the value remained stable.

Thus, as the majority of my clients had bought the stock at one dollar and only the latest had paid a little more, they were delighted when they heard that they had sold their shares at an average price of ten dollars and fifty cents.

Their profit was enormous.

My dramatic results earned me the respect and admiration of all, but for me, the relief of having a narrow escape was much more significant. I could not help but think with anxiety that, if they had been impatient or if the share price had stagnated, I surely would not have received their praise. They would probably have lost a lot of money overnight ... I had a chill down my back.

I made a promise never to work in this kind of brokerage firm again and no longer touch the penny-stocks, even if these instruments were not prohibited by law. I was lucky and so were my clients.

I never knew what happened to the biotech company, but the idea was good ...

In fact, a few years later the little blue pill appeared with its notorious success.

D.K. (Don't Know)

The ladder of success is best climbed by stepping on the rungs of opportunity.

—*Ayn Rand*

In one of the largest investment banks on Wall Street, no more commissions of thousands of dollars accounted for half the amount paid by the customer. I had to earn my wages gradually.

It was always better to sell the products of my company but I no longer had the obligation to do so. The methods proved more ethical, the choices were many and the proposed values seemed safer.

I gave myself a few weeks to find a suitable new investment in order to offer my clients a pertinent way to reinvest their money. I preferred to wait for an opportunity, leaving them time to rejoice over their earnings and talk about them. Actually, I was not sure if I could keep performing for them, knowing that the phenomenal growth of their assets could not be repeated, and that my reputation could suffer as a result.

While other brokers thought only about selling, I was looking for a solid investment but, as was the custom in every brokerage firm, it was necessary to open new accounts. To do this, I had to call people from a list of prospects and persuade them to trust me and buy stocks. These were to be selected by myself, without any influence from my superiors and it was up to me to find an attractive purchase, but it was not so easy.

Once a person called on the phone agreed to acquire a number of shares, the opening formalities were to note their name, date and place of birth, address, social security number and income. A short questionnaire on the value of their assets was completed and the order was taken. I then had the paperwork signed by my boss and I placed the order. Once executed, the price was given to the client, so he could send a check for payment.

Not rocket science. Since the beginning of my career as a broker, no one had caused me any problem.

One morning, I opened a new account for an old woman who had accepted with enthusiasm my recommendation on a stock offering good dividends. Because of her age, I preferred to advise a stock with solid value and I proposed Chevron (CVX). Once her order was completed, I called her back a few minutes later and gave her the confirmation.

The next day at the opening of the market, she called me on the phone to ask the price of the stocks she had just bought. I answered without hesitation:

"CVX down 50 cents today to $52, in tandem with the Dow down 38 points."

I was hit by a torrent of screams, a tirade accusing me of having influenced her by my selling arguments. She did not want the stock and neither my firm nor I could force her to pay. If the case went to court, she continued, the judges would be on her side as she was very old.

All this was delivered so fluently that I had the impression this was not the first time she had reacted in such a way!

I was stunned and could not believe what I was hearing. Nevertheless, I found the words to answer respectfully and without losing my composure:

"Are you sure, Madam? This investment is one of the safest of the market. It appears in the most conservative portfolios and ..."

She cut me off very sharply, to repeat emphatically that she would not pay.

Without insisting more, I reassured her politely

"Very well Madam, don't worry. I am taking care of it immediately and closing your account. I'm sorry."

This was the only D.K. in my career (Don't Know - When a client ignores a transaction). After consulting the Litigation Department, who confirmed my fears, I called the orders desk to reverse the position. Chevron was still at the same price and I knew I would have to pay out of my pocket the 50 cents loss multiplied by the thousand shares ordered the previous day.

Thinking, after all, that it was an occupational hazard, I faced my responsibility without complaining. Obviously, it was a miracle that this had not happened to me at Hamilton-Grant! In hindsight, I realized what a nightmare it would have been there.

After this incident, I began to look more closely at some of the tools that the best performing brokers used. I discovered that it was possible to entrust the responsibility for my accounts to experienced managers who would pay me a commission every time they carried out a transaction in the portfolios of my clients.

To do this, I chose the best PM (Portfolio Managers) based on their results over one, five and ten years and advised my clients to invest with them. When shares were purchased or sold by these managers, the execution fees would automatically be credited to me.

This new way of doing my job allowed me to make sales without having myself a thorough knowledge of the secrets of Wall Street. I was unaware of the reason behind a quote going up after bad news sometimes, or drop in price after the release of pretty good results. To my logical mind, this was incomprehensible.

However, if I still had no idea about what could cause these unexpected reactions, I really intended to learn.

I just needed a little time.

"TAKE CONTROL OF YOUR MONEY"

You have to be constantly reinventing yourself and investing in the future.

—Reid Hoffman (LinkedIn)

My office was located on Park Avenue.

Widows or divorced women accounted for a large part of my book and, even if my appearance was too young for them to trust me, they were reassured by the results and experience of the portfolio manager who was going to grow their wealth, through my introduction.

Few of them could decide for themselves what tools to use and how to invest their assets. Financial issues had probably been the responsibility of their former husbands and they were a bit overwhelmed by the burden of taking over.

Their candor and questions about money matters gave me the idea of hosting free seminars every Tuesday evening in the conference room of my office, to teach them about the various investments.

"Take Control of Your Money" became very popular and allowed me to expand my clientele. Thanks to these weekly meetings, more and more people recommended me to their friends. Thus, my financial situation was improving rapidly.

However, I was determined to get all the additional qualifications which could open up some doors in the future and I kept going to night classes in order to add to my existing licenses, those of commodity trading and stock trading.

I also read a lot.

To begin, I devoured the best writings published by the most famous investors, with the hope of finding everything I might need to fast track my career.

To this reading, I added the study of psychology. This subject fascinated me and after having sifted through a good twenty books on behavior analysis to better understand people, I lingered especially on Neuro-Linguistic Programming (NLP), in order to communicate better with others. In addition, I studied all the works of renowned authors to improve individual development. Dale Carnegie and Napoleon Hill were on the top of my list and I discovered new ones at the time, like Stephen Covey, whose book on the *Seven Habits of Highly Effective People* was just published.

Besides, I also taught my children some details about what I learned. I considered the information extremely important for their personal development and I used these references in order to assist them in their intellectual growth. With my desire to instill this knowledge in my boys, I was hoping to give them the best possible chance of success.

My job as a parent was to guide them on the path to a bright future and I intended to show them a good example.

"Women of Wall Street"

*Think like a queen. A queen is not afraid to fail.
Failure is another steppingstone to greatness.*

—*Oprah Winfrey*

I had had no news about the publication of "Women of Wall Street" and I prayed to God that this edition of Playboy would never appear. But one evening when I got home, I found a letter with this announcement:

"Congratulations, you are about to be famous!"

In the envelope was also a photocopy of the article with my photos. Even though they only showed one nipple and they were quite artistic, I was horrified ... Exposing myself in this way was not at all the image that my clients, my company or my colleagues would expect of me.

It was a disaster!

All evening, I thought about the consequences of these images and I was upset. My situation was very different from when I posed, because now I had a real job. Over time, I had innocently hoped that the draft publication would be canceled and I could escape this dilemma, but now I knew I would have to pay for my misjudgment.

After a sleepless night rehashing all the inevitable repercussions, I was unable to go to work that morning.

How was I going to tell my director that a young mom with impeccable manners and respected by all, as was my case, had dared to undress for Playboy? How to explain that I had done that before holding my current position and that it was on the advice of my boss, a year earlier?

Whatever my reasons, the facts were there and no one was going to take my excuses into account.

I could certainly be fired ... And how would I provide for my sons, who got used to having their own bedroom. Could I find another job?

The children were at camp and I was left alone in the apartment, tortured by these thoughts, when the phone rang. A woman affiliated with the CBS television network, said she had an agreement with the publisher of Playboy. Immediately, I hoped to convince her to help me, figuring it was not too late to prevent the publication of my pictures. She asked me many questions about the circumstances that made me accept and, undaunted, I emptied my bag without understanding exactly where she was going...

But at the end of the conversation, she told me that a movie called "I Posed for Playboy" would be shot with actress Lynda Carter where my story would be featured.

I was stunned, thinking it had to be a misunderstanding ... But no! I had talked too much and unfortunately my situation had worsened.

Ashamed and disappointed, I expected the worst.

The next day, I knocked on my director's door and placed the letter I had received on his desk, saying simply:

"I'm really sorry!"

After taking a look at the contents, he raised his eyebrows and looked at me incredulously, as if he had received a shock. After a moment, he whispered:

"No! Not you?"

He was visibly annoyed and shook his head negatively. After a deep sigh, he asked me to return to my desk and when I turned to leave, he added, terribly upset:

"We'll talk later!..."

Bodyguard and Limousine

The best protection any woman can have... is courage.

—*Elizabeth Cady Stanton*

The same evening, two senior officials came to my office and brought me to the headquarters by limousine.

There, after hearing my explanation of what had happened, they gave me the assurance that my job was not in danger. However, they asked me to move into an office located on the same floor as the CEO in the building on Sixth Avenue, just to be safe for the time being.

I was informed that during the next two months, or until the case was forgotten, a bodyguard would accompany me everywhere and keep my door day and night. I also learned that the same car and driver we just used, would be at my disposal 24/7.

They needed me to agree only to one condition: Do not talk to the press.

Without hesitation, I accepted immediately. A year had passed and my perspective was totally different than when I worked at Hamilton-Grant. My decision to pose had been taken in the hope to live more comfortably, but my situation had greatly improved without the publicity. Now, instead of helping me, this misstep could destroy my career and reputation.

I sincerely regretted it...

The few weeks spent at the head office were no problem. The only thing that was a little shocking was that I had to be accompanied by a lady to go to the bathroom. Obviously, the management did not joke about the fact that I could be asked questions there, as well as anywhere.

Some time later, my life returned to normal and I went back to my office on Park Avenue where a mountain of gifts and fan mail were waiting for me. Having no wish to have them in my office, I had it all delivered to my apartment but, contrary to what I had imagined, the presents received in my absence could have been for a bookseller or a teacher.

The many admirers sent stylish scarves, subscriptions to financial magazines and the Smithsonian museum, books on finance ... etc. Cover letters were friendly and polite, but I did not answer any. I was eager to erase this episode from my memory and I had no intention of mentioning anything about it to anyone. But ultimately, I was deeply relieved to be treated in an appropriate manner by all these people. I had dreaded receiving hints or vulgar innuendo and it was not the case at all. I was addressed with respect, which was both surprisingly reassuring and pleasant.

Another surprise, new clients would contact me without any solicitation, without knowing me or telling me why, simply expressing a desire to open an account and buy some shares. Improbable yet true, there were people who, just because they found me attractive in a magazine, had chosen me for their broker.

Playboy had not only published my pictures, some wearing lingerie and another wearing a suit, cross-legged in front of the New York Stock Exchange, but the article which accompanied my portrait, based on my first interview with the journalist.

Despite not having been in contact since that time, the writer had discovered where I was now working, at the time of publication and the name of this large investment bank was highlighted. In the report, a comment revealed that, when I had previously been the employee of another company, I had advised my clients to buy a stock at one dollar and sold it for them at $10.50 six months later.

Of course, it was true but I wondered how he had found out. In any case, this story earned me many new customers and it was nice.

However, this increased attention also aroused the jealousy of some of my colleagues. On my desk were two frames: one picture showed my children and on the other I posed with the mayor of New York during the bicentennial celebration of the United States Constitution. One morning, the glass of the frame representing me with Mayor Koch was broken and on a sheet of paper next to it, the word "whore" was written in red marker.

In panic I called my manager, who came right away. After looking at my desk without a word, he went back to his office to announce on the microphone that he wanted all employees to come in the conference room, immediately!

Before all the staff, he growled in a threatening voice that if anyone, even the most famous broker in the firm, dared to insult me or to make an unpleasant remark about me, this person would be fired.

I was sad to learn that the affable face of one of my colleagues was a facade. I never found out who was responsible.

Fortunately, the incident was soon forgotten.

My monthly performance soared and I won several trophies to reward my sales growth, including a clock "L'Epée" of great value.

Visit to a Hedge Fund

If you live among wolves you have to act like a wolf.

—*Nikita Khrushchev*

My excellent results had led me to meet traders who were interested in my IPO allocation for their hedge fund.

Since I had a solid customer base, I was entitled to a greater amount of securities when IPOs were issued, a number growing with my business. Knowing that each dealer could not give more than a certain quantity of shares per account, traders sought to have brokers at as many different firms as possible, and hence the interest of these funds to do business with me.

Moreover, to prove that they were active, they gave me regular orders of at least ten thousand shares, without any solicitation on my part. While they were paying me great commissions, they were able to get the maximum attributed on the "hot" IPOs.

At the time, new issues opened up sharply on their first day of issuance and getting as much as possible could be very profitable. The professionals indicated a very impressive total number of shares to buy while the allocation to be delivered by the sales executive depended on the size of his business.

Thus, the best customers of the best brokers were favored, without exceeding the limit.

Unlike all conventional investment funds, which were closely monitored and had to meet rigid regulations, hedge funds were almost uncontrolled and quite rare at that time; they were only for investors whose assets amounted to several million dollars.

Another feature of these alternative investment funds was that they could capitalize on the weakness of a market and gain on shares or indices that lost their value.

They also used "leverage", which was a technique to multiply gains (or losses). This meant incurring a huge debt by borrowing money at a lower interest rate and then using the excess funds in high-risk investments to maximize returns. These loans were made automatically by the clearing house after the fund had opened a margin account or a futures account.

The most obvious danger of leverage was to multiply losses as easily as profits. The greater the leverage, the faster positions up against the market could lose and unless the trader cut his losses rapidly, it entailed serious problems.

For the trading of securities, if an investor had bought shares "on margin", which was set at 50% at that time, a price reduction of 20% represented a loss of 40%.

In alternative investments, many transactions were done with options and futures, which had the effects of infinitely greater leverage. Futures were trading tools that showed the expected price of an instrument at a certain date in the future. The difference between the "leverage" of futures and that of shares traded was remarkable and traders of a hedge fund had to be experts, since the risks were multiplied.

With experience and a good risk management, this leverage was used to obtain more profits, while using a minimal capital. The debt (leverage) on futures was by far the most important and the danger was that 100% of the initial deposit (the amount required to enter into a trade) could be lost if the market went against the position by only 2 or 3%.

The futures market, where instruments on all commodities, indexes, government bonds and currencies were traded, was often used by hedge funds, since they favored those with the greatest leverage. Providing ample liquidity and volatility, futures were great tools for traders, whether they were very short-term (day-trading), swing traders (who kept positions for a few days) or hedgers, trading for a longer term. The latter were producers of a commodity, wanting to secure a selling price today for the products they would issue at a later date.

Traders at a hedge fund had to have an excellent understanding of the market they traded and know how to use these instruments, but thanks to their high leverage, they were among the most profitable financial tools, although potentially the most dangerous, since there was always a balance of risk and reward.

The methods used by these funds had to be based on a very sound strategy. In the case of large losses, if the "margin" (minimum deposit required by the exchange) was hit or exceeded, the position was closed without asking the trader's permission by the "Margin Clerks". These were employees of the clearing house and they had a duty to monitor accounts for any position exceeding the required capital.

Naturally, the only people able to work with these tools were professional traders who knew their job and how to avoid the disasters that leverage could bring.

These hedge funds also used options, which offered as much leverage as futures, although their liquidity was rarely large enough as they lack the necessary volume for size orders. Therefore, the "spread" (the difference between bid and offer) on options was often very large. They carried increased risks with the erosion of their value over time (time value) and they would often behave with a frightening volatility.

The "spreads" of the options were a bit like those penny-stocks in which Hamilton-Grant made a market.

I was intrigued by the activity of my clients' traders and I decided to visit their office, which was close to the New York Stock Exchange.

Immediately, I was struck by the intensity of the atmosphere on the trading desk where some of the men stood up abruptly, waving their arms as if to give more strength to their words. Their aggression was in the air and I was a little surprised to hear a profanity inserted between each word, as they shouted orders over the phone.

No women worked there. The ambient rage and wild gestures really made an impression on me.

All these men with rude manners seemed to be rabid, and they were not kidding. They looked like hungry wolves looking for a prey.

But whatever their ways, one thing was certain: they earned a lot of money. Rolex at their wrist, sports car or Rolls in the garage, they seemed to be part of an elite clan. The majority of them were not even thirty years old.

Looking at their behavior, I could not help thinking that if they could do this job, I'd be able to do it too, if only I could study their tactics ...

Quite determined to find out more, I went to visit them regularly. The more I discovered, the more I wanted to learn how to perform their work. The problem was there was no school that taught how to make money by trading. My "Series 55" license gave me permission to trade stocks actively, but what I had learned for my graduation was far from what was practiced on the desk.

Despite this, a phrase kept running through my head:

"When we want, we can."

This sentence was written above the blackboard in my class when I was a little girl and these few words remained embedded in my memory, inspiring my life.

Since I had amassed great savings, I decided to make an appointment with Mr. Townsend, the owner of the hedge fund. He was a tall man, approaching middle age and dressed with impeccable style. His short graying hair made him appear stern and his extremely white face gave him a sickly look. He had nodded towards me at each of my visits, but it was the first time I had an appointment.

When he sat down in the small conference room to hear the reason of this meeting, his steely eyes stared at me coldly, as if he wanted to read what I was going to say even before I started talking to him. Bravely, I asked him if he would accept me as his assistant, without pay for six months. He let me speak without interrupting me while I explained my intention of learning the trade.

After a moment that seemed like forever, he frowned in puzzlement.

For a time he just looked me in the eyes, thoughtful and serious, without saying a word. As for me, I was frozen, fearing his refusal. I did not even dare to breathe. Although I was hoping with all my heart that he accepted, I could see no real reason why he should.

Finally, his face lit up and he seemed relaxed and entertained at the same time. He smiled and, to my surprise, he agreed.

Was it because he wanted to see how fast I would give up, or for the sake of having a "Playboy Bunny" at his side for a week or two before firing me? ...

I had no idea.

However, I considered his answer as a total victory. A wave of happiness came over me and I felt a door had just opened on my destiny. I knew it was the beginning of a great journey that would surely put me to the test, and I was not scared. I was even anticipating the challenge eagerly.

On a handshake, he asked me to come at eight o'clock the first Monday of the following month. For me, it was all that mattered. I promised him he would not be disappointed and would not regret his decision.

Back at the office, I went to my manager immediately and told him about my desire to take a sabbatical year, informing him of my plans to become trader in a hedge fund. He said he was sorry for my departure, and if I ever wanted to return to be a broker, he would be happy to have me back.

It was reassuring and I knew that his words were sincere. He wished me luck and, happily, I kissed him on the cheek and thanked him.

An adventure was about to begin; it was up to me to build a bright future.

After all, I had faith, I was young and I knew that my dream was possible. My decision was made and I was determined to learn this business, whatever it cost me.

To celebrate the good news, I called my best friend Lila and asked her to meet me for lunch the next day, in a popular cafe in South Street Seaport. She was a pretty brunette, born in Brooklyn and was just twenty years old. Before going back to school, she was in an internship at Tudor Investment Corp., a well-known hedge fund.

Her boss, Paul Tudor Jones, had been a broker before becoming a portfolio manager like Mr. Townsend.

People said that ten years earlier, when he was about to enroll at Harvard Business School, he realized that no school, however famous, could teach him the secrets learnt on an exchange. So instead, he went to the New York Cotton Exchange where he was trained by a renowned trader.

After that, he opened his own fund and became famous for winning a fortune on the day of the 1987 crash.

FIRST DAY

Control your own destiny or someone else will.

—*Jack Welch*

From when I had first started on Wall Street, I was accustomed to go to work dressed in an elegant suit, worn over a silk blouse. For my learning among traders, I added a tie, which I wore on a more masculine shirt in order to be dressed like the others, at least from the neck to the waist. That way, I felt I was part of the clan, although I wore a skirt, stockings and high heels.

The first day, when I arrived Mr. Townsend asked me to take the seat next to him. To mimic the traders who took off their jackets before sitting down, I removed mine too and hung it on the back of my chair. He immediately asked me to register at the New York Institute of Finance to study Technical Analysis in evening classes.

It was imperative!

Fortunately, the course began a new session that week and I enrolled right away, while he was taking calls from brokers. Before the market opened, all the major investment banks provided guidance on the recommendations of their analysts. Their brokers informed customers about what securities they would negotiate during the day and which blocks of shares would be offered. If one of the traders was interested, he just indicated at what price he was a taker and for what amount.

Between two telephone conversations, Mr. Townsend handed me an invitation to attend a gala dinner for large traders in his place, suggesting that it was useful to meet people in the business, apart from on the trading desk.

After thanking him, I looked at the screen where a sign was stuck, with the words:

"No Emotion = Discipline!"

I did not know that this little phrase was the perfect description of the attitude necessary for trading. Since that day, I have found none other that can better suit, even after many years of trading.

He showed me his "blotter" (register) where all his transactions were entered and he gave me a small booklet in which to write some of the principles he considered essential to remember.

Immediately, I learned some fascinating facts.

When a huge bid was displayed and the offer was minimal in comparison, if the bid suddenly disappeared, the chart indicated whether this exchange had been performed or not, with the behavior of the volume. If it was just a ruse to try to attract buyers by exhibiting a large purchase order, this fact was revealed by the volume not having increased.

Whether the order was true or false, if the price fell rapidly after the disappearance of the bid, the buyer "at the market", which was influenced by the trap of a large buy order, had certainly lost money.

Looking at several time-frames of a chart (time differences ranging from less than a minute to a month), allowed the trader to read and understand the trend of a market more clearly. The trading strategy had to be adapted to whichever graph interval seemed to be the most profitable, according to the trader's own style.

Over the days, only the activity of Mr. Townsend was essential to me. I ignored the other traders and I was determined to take advantage of my apprenticeship. This was my chance and I did not want to waste it.

My detachment intrigued my colleagues. A woman on the desk was unusual and they were probably betting on the longevity of my presence in this den of wild beasts.

As for me, I focused on my training and ignored their shouting and swearing. As long as they were not addressed to me, I was indifferent to their cursing. I kept my distance with all the men of the desk, even those who had been my clients and had got my IPO allocations.

Gradually, I started to earn the respect of many. No doubt some of them had read the magazine article and saw me partly undressed in it, but nobody mentioned it in front of me and my serious demeanor disassociated me totally with that detail. They knew I was applying myself so my education was thorough and effective.

I was determined to find out how to proceed to make money, to adopt what did work and avoid what did not work. I understood the need to be in the right place at the right time and, of course, to trade with the trend of the market to win. Indeed, I had to study the methods that would allow me to find this right combination of timing and direction and I was counting on the technical analysis tools.

At the New York Institute of Finance, my classes were taught by a great professor. With simple explanations and a humorous association to every major rule, this analyst had the skill to turn these hours of class into absolutely exciting moments. Previously, it would have seemed insane to me to attempt to predict the price of a share in advance and yet, I discovered that it was possible.

More than a science, it was an art.

As the basis of technical analysis was revealed to me, the price reflected the actual value, and the display of the quote was justified by the sum of all the information and knowledge. Therefore, the price showing revealed the current assessment. The study of charts with their trend, support, resistance and other calculations allowed traders to predict the future movement of the price and was used to identify opportunities for potential profit.

Historical patterns repeated frequently and the value changed following a visible trend allowing professionals to anticipate the next move and to make a credible forecast.

Markets evolved according to supply and demand and orders were often motivated by fear or greed. An economic report meant nothing by itself and depended only on the interpretation of the mass of traders.

"A picture is worth a thousand words." The chart was the graphic expression of market sentiment.

A trader was able to get confirmation of the general trend quickly when looking at several time intervals of the graph of a stock. When the period considered was short (number of ticks per bar, one, five or ten minutes) a signal to buy or sell would be less effective and profitable, unless the position was kept in correlation to the time-frame analyzed. For example, when trading on a five minute chart, it was recommended to keep the trade open only for two or three times that period.

Thus, a buy signal obtained from a ten-minute graph was only effective for a maximum period of half an hour unlike a weekly signal, which required keeping the position for longer, with a stop farther from the entry point. On a long-term chart the profit potential was greater, as well as the risk.

Very short time charts often had a lot of "noise" caused by Scalpers (traders taking profits for pennies) or by small orders without consequences. Thus, a signal had more opportunities to appear, but it was less reliable. To verify the potential of a trade, an overview of a couple of longer time-frame graphs was necessary because buy or sell signals on very short intervals were quickly visible and canceled most of the time too. So the trader had to get out of his position, in accordance to the time interval chosen.

It was fascinating!

The majority of my evenings were spent studying and I waited for the weekend to really be with the children.

The quality of these moments was probably not sufficient and did not compensate for my long absence days, but I tried to make amends by little attentions and good quality time with them on weekends.

Yet exceptionally, the Saturday night of the invitation, I entrusted my children to my neighbor and went to the gala affair for traders.

I was sitting next to a gentleman named Bernie Madoff[1] who was obviously highly respected by all the other guests. During our conversation, I informed him of my desire to become a trader, to which he replied with kindness, that to succeed in this business, you just needed to "parlay the money".

I thanked him and noted the quote on his card. The evening was very informative through the lectures from different personalities addressing the audience on the future of the industry.

At that time, the obligations of my frantic race to success were many, but I did my best to be a caring mom, a responsible dad, and at the same time, to set a good example for the studies of my boys, so that they would grow up in the best way possible.

Luckily, I benefited from a strong will and great energy. Without a moment's respite, I was able to raise my children alone, monitor their homework, work on Wall Street and never miss an evening class, all without being entitled to unemployment compensation and without pay.

---

1 Bernard (Bernie) Madoff was the chairman of Nasdaq. However, eighteen years later, in December 2008, he was arrested by the FBI for making the scam of the century style "Ponzi" valued at 65 billion dollars. It seems ironic that his advice to me was to reuse the money, which is the basic principle of a "Ponzi scheme."

APPRENTICESHIP

Live as if you were to die tomorrow,
Learn as if you were to live forever.

—Mahatma Gandhi

In a few weeks, I was so effective that nothing was demanded of me, each task being already accomplished before being asked for.

While my help seemed to be appreciated, I was interested in every detail of the job and I did not hesitate to ask many questions, to which Mr. Townsend gave me short, logical and clear answers. In my eyes, he was a model trader who lived by the pulse of the market and I had a great admiration for this man.

I appreciated the chance of having him as my mentor.

Carefully, I studied his every move, his reactions, and what he watched. I tried to soak up the circumstances while imagining the movement of his thoughts.

Among the various instruments used by traders, futures, commodities, currencies, the choices were numerous but, on my trading desk, only the stocks of the New York Stock Exchange were traded.

Of course, before deciding on a position or considering interesting stocks, a trader should have chosen the market in which he would operate. For the best results, it was preferable that the exchange had the following attributes:

LIQUIDITY - Much interest and orders of size, to buy and to sell. It was one of the most important attributes for allowing a trader to enter or exit a position quickly.

EFFICIENCY - A market had to offer good executions, at the price of the quote. The broker taking the order had to be there, as otherwise the transaction must be made electronically.

LEVERAGE - If leverage was a danger to the uninitiated, it was an advantage for experienced operators, who used a solid risk management.

VOLATILITY - When the market was asleep, it was difficult to make money. Traders appreciated the large price movements, from which they profited.

Another important consideration was to take into account how markets often acted perversely and therefore, professionals should be able to adapt quickly to change. Indeed, it was during abnormal events that opportunities for gains could reward a trade entry by an amount equivalent to several weeks of benefits.

Undoubtedly, any trader had to consider the economic bulletins.

Regardless of whether the government figures were estimates, or based on data already received, the official information had a lot of weight on the financial markets' behavior. Although the results were often significantly revised, and this several times before a final conclusion could be published much later, reactions anticipating the future consequences were immediate.

Moreover, without departing purely from trading rules, it was imperative to examine the information to assess the country's prosperity, since this kind of warning dramatically affected the markets.

Every morning, investment banks announced their new recommendations. From when I first started on the trading desk of Mr. Townsend, I was accustomed to note the best securities mentioned and the general research affecting the stock market.

The observations that were made came from fundamental analysis, for example the evaluation of a company's financial statements and health when compared to other enterprises in the same sector.

Of course, this analysis was necessary for the positions kept long periods, but its timing often left something to be desired. This is why technical analysis was essential.

I worked diligently to improve my knowledge quickly. I was looking for methods taking into account several different analysis tools, so that I could soon be exercising my business in an efficient way that would allow me to get to a good performance in my short-term trading, at least I hoped.

Also, I felt the need to have an overview of the elements, to better understand what could affect the financial system. In order to progress with additional support, I discovered cycle analysis, a logically interesting study.

Undoubtedly, nature evolved by recurring periods. There was the cycle of the seasons, day and night, the phases of the moon, the migration of birds south, the hibernation of certain animals, salmon swimming upstream or dates conducive to mating for some races.

More importantly, I discovered that the secret to career success depended on psychology and the true victory of a trader was won after a struggle with himself.

Now, I guessed that emotions had negative repercussions on how people traded. The small label on Mr. Townsend's screen was there for a reason. No emotion equals discipline.

"Paper" trades (practice trades without money) did not generate the agitation and emotion associated with the value of the gain or loss because it was easy to keep the brain disciplined and act in accordance with all the rules, since the risks were not real.

Without capital commitment, decisions could be made without hesitation, while observing the planned strategy. Indeed, I practiced many "paper" trades and managed to do pretty well. However, the moment the bet was real, everything changed dramatically.

To keep a cool head and use fully one's capabilities, a good training was necessary and it was recommended to practice with very small sums at first, before increasing the value after 40 or 50 transactions, once a minimum of experience and confidence were somewhat acquired.

Obviously, each trader was different.

To determine his risk tolerance (and resilience to losses), the trader needed to know his own level of aggressiveness, his appetite for risk and his understanding of the market. In addition, his knowledge of the behavior of the security he was going to trade needed to be high. All this was necessary before committing.

If a person easily panicked and jumped up and down screaming or, on the contrary, became paralyzed and watched helplessly a loss getting bigger, these two opposites would not last long in the business.

Having a plan and following a strategy allowed traders to deal with circumstances with more confidence. The position must have been studied and planned previously, to allow the trader to stay confident. Thus, emotions did not come into play since the preparation had been made in advance. The trader had only to follow it with discipline to keep his composure.

What moved the markets were extreme emotions. A stock market crash happened only if all investors panicked in mass on the same day.

Fear and greed were the most common disorders.

The fear engendered mistakes, and greed just as much.

In general, any major excitement was bad for the trader because he could lose all or part of his ability to think. The time to jump for joy or sweat profusely would be deducted from the time to analyze the situation and would tax his ability to remain objective. This was the reason why the size of the positions was crucial.

A trader had to adapt to his own emotional comfort. Too large positions would prevent him from remaining calm and any surprise would make him ill.

According to the men on the trading desk, their reactions were quite different, when fear took hold of them. Some traders got sick; others shouted insults or, at the height of their anger, threw something with such fury as to break it.

Frustration and rage were other reactions leading to a regrettable blunder. When a trader felt defeated by an event or a person, frustrated by the idea of shortfall or enraged to have been duped, he was more likely to make additional errors.

The ego could also cause problems by influencing the trader to refuse to close a bad trade, not to lose face. If a trader clung to his position or attempted bad maneuvers to try to make up the lost money, he was bound to precipitate his capital into a fall of more serious value.

I learned that if the price did not behave as expected, it was enough to cut the position, respecting the principle that it is not only better to keep some dry powder in the gun for other attempts, but it also freed the mind. Otherwise, the trader remained fixated on this trade and would be unable to detect other opportunities.

Self-control and preparation were vital in this business and allowed an absence of concern, worry and emotion.

I had every intention of doing things in order. The first step was to learn the basics of trading and practice "on paper". For this, following the information and research of the investment banks, I noted on a sheet some fictitious transactions, which I was very proud of, because I had excellent results.

I felt sure that I was gifted in this field. Of course, the influence of my mentor played an important role, which is why I did not say anything. Thereafter, I would have the experience needed to negotiate for real in the most difficult kind of trading there is, day trading.

There were several styles.

A Position-Trader entered a trade for some time, often more than a week or a month, making his decisions based on fundamental analysis combined with technical analysis, in order to enter at the right time. It was advisable to start by position-trading, which was a bit like investing. Only after a number of profitable trades, when the trader was used to the principle, could another style be tried.

Intermediate, came the Swing Trader who conducted trades kept for a period of three to five days. This required a little more experience, which had often been acquired after having held a post of Position Trader.

Most advanced yet was the Short-Term Trader. The latter adopted a style of trading that, in addition to being difficult, was the most risky, requiring a formidable discipline. To become a day-trader (with positions kept for only a few minutes or a few hours), required a degree of excellence and, like an athlete, daily practice. It was the same principle requirement necessary for a pianist or a gymnast; to do it perfectly, it had to be done constantly.

If some people imagined that it was easy to do day trading, it was common that their dreams turn into nightmares. In fact, day-trading was not recommended without a rigorous training and some experience. It was a job requiring much study and the talent to do it well. But, in my trading room, day trading was king and I learned its techniques day after day.

I tried to follow the gaze of my mentor to detect what interested him on his screen and I drank in his words, trying to understand his intentions and his every thought.

On his screen, just underneath the quote of the market index, figured a list of symbols, gauging the "temperature" of the exchange that day. The NYSE TICK index, calculated the number of shares rising minus the declining ones in the general market and the TIKI was the same but only on the Dow Jones shares. The TRIN, also called Arms Index, reflected overall market sentiment with a low number for a higher market and high number for a lower one, 0.50 being very positive and 2.00 extremely negative. The VIX showed the options' volatility (S&P): a low number meant that optimism reigned while a high one signaled investors' fear. Finally, the A/D line level was formed by the difference between the total of stocks up and stocks down.

These internal market indicators were the most popular. Then, the study of graphs proved indispensable.

On the trading desk, an expression kept returning:

"THE TREND IS YOUR FRIEND."

This phrase of wisdom was the traders' favorite. When entering a position, observing the trend was considered like guiding a ship, with the wind in the sails.

The easiest method was to map the direction of the price trend with confirmation of its tilt on a higher time frame graph. Once the trendline was established, it was enough to add moving averages (MA) of 20 and 50 periods, and make sure they visibly followed the same path. The entry was made when the price extended its advance rapidly, away from its average, but came back to touch the MA20 line, and the signal to trade was a small bar or "candle" showing indecision, which indicated that the move backward was ending. The stop was placed on the passing of the same candle in reverse.

In addition, I learned that when a stock enjoyed a new yearly higher price, that is, higher than its top price of the last 52 weeks and it happened on a Friday when the market was about to close at the highest of the day (or near it), there was a tactic to purchase this security just before the closing time and to keep the position for the weekend.

The ploy was to sell the stock on Tuesday, when the market opened, which was usually a very profitable trade. But if the market opened significantly lower on Monday morning, it was necessary to get out of this trade immediately. This event was one of the few exceptions where a day-trader kept a position more than a day.

Another technique was to seek "inside days" (preferably on a daily chart) which meant a bar or candle located within the price range of the previous bar. This characteristic hesitation between buyers and sellers meant we had to buy if the price was above the little hesitation bar the next day and sell, if it was under.

Most traders preferred to work with candlesticks charts and each of them applied a strategy that suited him, according to his personality.

Because it was day-trading, some of the methods could be compared to "scalping" which meant getting out of the position as soon as it was profitable.

A system called "trend fading" meant to buy when the price had touched a price support and therefore, was undervalued, and to sell when a resistance was reached; hence an overvalued price level. Then, the momentum of a movement in one direction, accompanied with higher volume, was an indication of force which would influence the trader to enter in the same direction, after a slight pull back to "digest" the initial advance.

Lots of strategies were used for pivot points, which were calculated from the previous day and would provide both levels of support and resistance. As for the protective stop, each method used was to include a rule stating its location.

I felt confident that I was mastering the techniques of disciplined trading by following carefully Mr. Townsend's every move, but I soon realized that there could be surprises.

One day, when a stock was particularly bearish, Mr. Townsend received a call from a broker asking him if he wanted to participate in a block purchase, two points lower.

"I'm game for 100," (100,000 shares) he replied without hesitation.

I was startled, since the graph did not yet support his answer and his answer did not correspond to his habits, as there was no indication of recovery. But he explained that when a price has been seriously down and confirmed by its decreasing slope line for a long time, then a new low price was reported (a candle representing a lower low) with huge volume, it was a circumstance to consider more closely.

It was possible and even probable, that a seller of a very large amount, who had worked his order for weeks, ended his entire position with a final block. Most often, this exchange was agreed with an investment bank that took all his inventory off him, at a sold off level.

This was a sign that the seller had ended his lot by winding it up and, most likely, the pressure on the stock would be reduced or even disappear.

In addition, there was a good chance that the investment bank would decide to publish a positive research report on the stock, a few days after acquiring the batch. This report would praise its value and its attractive price and the bank could sell the entire amount to its customers, and get out of its recent acquisition with profits on its purchase.

For the trader, it was also a signal that the stock had finished falling as relentlessly, and finally, it was likely to rise as the pressure was removed, at least temporarily. Thus, upon the publication of the research, Mr. Townsend would sell his shares, recording a good gain.

I recognized that even once I had mastered the tools and the graphs, there was still plenty to learn about trading! I felt very grateful that I had found such a fine teacher.

I also learned that operators were attentive to price differentials, which one day or the other would be filled. It was commonly accepted that the value should be negotiated at every price of a chart and that an open "gap", left after a stock had jumped in value, should be filled in most cases.

However, the common point of each true professional was to make the least possible errors.

The goal was not to be a genius and to find the perfect instrument; on the contrary, it was to accept that the job was made of profits and losses, while trying to get more income and less risk.

Recognizing quickly that an entry had been too early or too late, and had missed its potential benefit, was a great mental development that had to be acquired in order to get to a winning mindset. The key was to profit on the total number of transactions, without worrying if some had not performed as expected.

Therefore, I had to focus my attention on a good discipline and on the tools that could have the most impact in my analysis. While allowing me a regular performance, it was a needed condition to exercise my future job with talent, as a day-trader.

At least I hoped.

On the trading desk, I heard phrases of common sense and from time to time, I took note of those that seemed paramount, and so my notebook filled:

- ✓ Technical analysis is a windsock, not a crystal ball. It is a skill that improves with experience and time. We need to study it, because there is always someone smarter than us. Price reveals the truth.

- ✓ We cannot control the market. The best thing to do is try to understand what the market is trying to say.

- ✓ Most traders take a good system and destroy it, by trying to turn it into a perfect system.

- ✓ Sell when you can, not when you need to.

- ✓ Learn to take your losses quickly and learn from your mistakes. Do not expect to be right all the time.

- ✓ Even a dead fish can go with the flow. However, it takes a strong fish to swim against the current. The opposite of courage is conformity; in other words, what seems to be a "difficult" choice at the time, has a potential for higher profits.

- ✓ "Hope" can be detrimental to your financial assets.

- ✓ Do not let a profitable trade turn into a loss; and, never let a trade become an investment, because it is a loss.

- ✓ There is no smoke without fire and when you see one cockroach, there are always many more. This means that bad news never comes alone; more will follow over time.

- ✓ It's not the investments that you sell and which continue to go higher without you that count, it's the ones you do not sell and which continue to lose value.

- ✓ Any small loss is part of the investment process. The key is not to let it become a big loss, which could devastate your portfolio.

- ✓ You must trade what you see, not what you think.

✓ All great traders share the same characteristic; they have the ability to change when events indicate change.

✓ Experienced traders control risk; those who are inexperienced chase profits.

FIBONACCI & ELLIOTT

Mathematics would certainly have not come into existence
if one had known from the beginning that there was in nature
no exactly straight line, no actual circle, no absolute magnitude.

—Friedrich Nietzsche

Trading, as it was practiced at Mr. Townsend's, was based on the basic principle that an established trend should continue its momentum, unless indicators showed a divergence with the price. The key was to determine at what level to enter, after a price had moved away from its moving average and once it had returned to an equilibrium. The signal of a return to the previous direction had to be visible in order to anticipate, with the best chances possible, that the decline was over.

This was particularly vital when markets were very volatile.

One of the best tools for calculating the percentage of the retracement came from an evidence found in nature and made famous eight centuries ago.

Leonardo of Pisa (aka Fibonacci) lived between 1170 and 1250 and was an Italian mathematician known for his books on arithmetic and geometry. To calculate the population growth of rabbits, he used a method using 0 and 1 as the first two numbers of a sequence, and each subsequent number being the sum of the previous two.

$$0 +1 = 1 +1 = 2 +1 = 3 +2 = 5 +3 = 8 +5 = 13 +8 = 21... \text{ etc..}$$

Fibonacci's name was later given to the evolutionary series. The interesting detail is that the quotient of one number, with respect to the previous one, remains the same and the ratio with the following number is also identical, regardless of the number in question, starting from the third. In addition, it has been shown that nature often has a growth rate using the same ratio, 1.618, which is called the "Golden Ratio". The expansion of the Nautilus shell is often cited as a perfect example.

Among an infinity of other examples, a sunflower forms two sets of spirals rotating in the opposite direction, their number in each case corresponding to two consecutive terms of the Fibonacci suite, as 34/55 or 55/89.

After the first few ones, the ratio of a number relative to the previous in the sequence is very close to the 1.618 marking an expansion and the ratio to the next higher number is almost 0.618 to represent a contraction. With a longer sequence the ratio approximated phi, an irrational number 0.618034 ...

Among other numbers in order, the quotient of a number placed ahead of the previous one was about 2.618 and inversely in relation to the one shown after the next, it was 0.382.

I soon mastered the mathematics of this and was enthralled to find how it could be used to make money.

In trading, the evolution of growth was often shown with a progression of 1.618% and a regression with a decrease of 0.618%. The turn of a price action was often demonstrated as being governed by the Golden Ratio, and Fibonacci appeared frequently in market statistics. The decline in the price on a graph often stopped in an area between 50 and 61.8% of the initial momentum.

Moreover, even if the numbers themselves had only a theoretical weight in the concept of movements formed, it was crucial to understand that this ratio was also the fundamental key to the study of growth models.

Nature used the Golden Ratio in its building blocks, in both the most intimate and its most advanced models, whether in the form of a tiny atomic structure, the molecules of the brain microtubules and DNA, or those much larger, the comets, planets and galaxies. This quotient was involved in phenomena as diverse as planetary distances and orbits, crystal formations, reflections of light beams on the glass, the brain and nervous system, musical arrangement, and also the structure of plants and animals.

Science showed that there was indeed a proportional base principle in nature.

Another study looked into nature and added psychology. I was still continuing to read books on this subject, not only because human behavior fascinated me, but also because of its importance in the behavior of the markets.

The Elliott wave principle was the discovery of Ralph Nelson Elliott, who described how the emotions of the masses had thrusts and setbacks, signaled by recognizable patterns.

Good market timing depended on the study of human behavior.

The principle of the Elliott waves considered that the evolution or the ever-changing path of stock prices (or any other instrument) was designed so as to reveal a structural concept reflecting a fundamental harmony, found also in nature. In a broad sense, the theory hypothesizes that the same law that shapes living creatures and galaxies influences the emotions and activities of men en masse.

Whatever the period analyzed on a chart, the price could be recognized as being in a particular level of a repetitive pattern of waves, whether they were motive (five waves) or corrective (three waves). A full cycle was then made of eight waves. Being able to identify the price position in a graph allowed the trader to trade with more conviction.

Considering these levels was useful. This study represented an additional tool that, in combination with other analyses, improved the chances of successful trading decisions.

In Charting, the price retracements that take the form of waves are often stopped at Fibonacci levels before resuming their trend. Traders used them regularly and it seemed perfectly natural to me to consider them.

To involve my children, every lunchtime on weekends, I left my real estate agency and took them to Central Park to find examples that showed natural growth in specific proportion.

Together we went to gather leaves, flowers or pine cones, which seemed to advance using this development principle, before having a picnic outdoors, when the time permitted. It was an excuse to get together. Since the change in value of the markets I was studying was close to the pace of growth in nature, they helped me with a little treasure hunt, to find the most possible samples.

Even if I had to go back to work in the afternoon, to try to sell or rent apartments, we still had our little family time.

Planning a Trade

First ask yourself: What is the worst that can happen?
Then prepare to accept it. Then proceed to improve on the worst.

—*Dale Carnegie*

The theory supporting a trend following position started from the assumption that the direction was well established and that it would continue its momentum.

In an uptrend, following a good move upward, it was necessary to wait until a price pull back, when the value had retraced enough of the advance to reach a level where buyers wanted to monopolize it again. This trade was then justified by the confirmation of a significant amount of evidence, outlined in the strategy.

The principle of an entry against the trend was that the latter was denied by a series of signs that reflected a weakening of the established direction and predicted a reversal of price, starting with a divergence of indicators.

Of course, each method had a special trigger signal and the position entry was governed by a set of rules to follow. These rules imposed the conditions and the location of the stop.

Whatever the tactic, if all the elements were not complete, the trade should not be placed. Thus, all the circumstances required had to be satisfied to anticipate making profits.

The goal was not to be right, but to execute the plan perfectly!

Performance should be considered on the general result of trading and not with the assumption that each of the trades would generate revenue. The aim was therefore to make regular gains over time, which allowed a positive P & L (profit and loss) overall, growing the portfolio's value.

To do this, it was essential to respect an established program, which listed the requirements stipulating the standards of the chosen strategy.

The transaction entry was justified by several reasons written in the plan and, if even only one of them became suspect, it was necessary to get out of the position immediately.

"When in doubt, get out!" This expression appeared to be a matter of safety, very simply.

Even if the trade could earn more, it was vital to meet the planning previously studied, which was done before the emotions of the market would interfere. As always, the trader had to stay disciplined and his preparation had to have been built so that the trade would avoid the least possible hazard, in order to limit the risks.

The calculation also had to include a stop, allowing the automatic exit of a trade before it could turn into a major loss, and to ensure this, it was essential to know where to place it. The objective was capital preservation before targeting an increase in its value and it was necessary to ensure that losses were kept minimal, compared to the size of the account.

Clearly, the fundamental basis of the business was to always have a potential gain greater than the potential loss (risk / return).

Failing to comply with the system of preparation because of a lack of discipline was the best way to increase the risk of getting into problems. Yet, even if this proved clear, it was the reason for 90% of failures among traders. Again and again I saw cases where emotion took over; a sure path to failure.

The key to success was to take small profits, regular and numerous, which would help the trader to have confidence in himself and, at the same time, would benefit the health of his portfolio. In the case of an asset manager, a constant yield was more attractive to investors than results that were too volatile.

More than anything, it was the habit of taking repeated gains that led the operator on the road to success. And, for this fidelity of results, it was necessary to have made the study, to have verified the calculations and to have prepared them in advance.

Planning his trades and trading his plan was the driver to attain success in this business.

What separated the great masters from all other traders was that the experts all had great patience. They preferred to wait and to make sure there were many reasons that piled up on top of each other, before deciding to enter a transaction.

Thus, what might seem a waste of time by repeated analyzes was, on the contrary, a way to get increased opportunities for victories. When the trades were considered and they offered a number as large as possible of probabilities, the portfolio was more likely to grow in value.

Since the strategies gave a list of rules, any preparation was incomplete if every condition mentioned in that list was not followed closely.

I had learnt early on the need for complete discipline. If I were to be successful in providing for my children, it had to become second nature to me to apply this to my career as a potential trader.

As for the strategy I used to raise my boys, I never scolded without giving a long explanation of what was right or wrong and I always did it with affection. I was not among those who advocated spanking, although many parents defended the argument that it was necessary.

My philosophy was to encourage them to be responsible for their actions, at an early age. To do that, I'd give them pocket money they could use at their discretion, to buy what they liked. However, each misbehavior was taxed by a puncture of the weekly amount due to them, and it could be completely removed if I judged their behavior terribly bad or if they did not deserve an allowance for having a disappointing school report card.

So I taught them early how to behave like big boys.

They had to deal with their duties and obligations, but were rewarded by a larger amount if they had done particularly well, in the same way an adult would have to pay for a ticket or an additional tax but could also receive a bonus, according to his conduct.

Risk Management

If you take no risks, you will suffer no defeats.
But if you take no risks, you win no victories.

—*Richard M. Nixon*

All strategies and formulas, as elaborate as they were, could not replace a good risk management, without which most traders were doomed to failure. Professionals had an expression for the fact that lack of caution was a good way to squander money, saying only half kiddingly:

"Without proper risk management, the only way to end up with a small fortune is to have started with a large one."

Disregarding contingencies and betting too big, from the first transactions, would be harmful and would dilapidate the account quickly, seriously compromising the longevity of the practice of the trade.

While some considered the risk as a percentage of the value invested, others ciphered it relative to the maximum dollar amount they accepted to lose. As for me, with my hope of becoming a trader in the near future, I planned to set my exposure based on the location of my stop, which was always placed at a level closely studied. Then, I would stagger my exits so my trade could be safe, by getting out of half the position as soon as it reached breakeven.

According to veterans, that not only helped to gain a better performance, but it made it possible to focus on other transactions, with less potential hazards.

This choice seemed easier to manage as it allowed a greater number of securities to be traded and followed mentally.

In trading from charts, the danger turned out to be the point where the assumption that had been made at the time of the trade entry was denied. Since that entry point had also dictated the stop level, caution was required.

On my trading desk, there were two favored trend-following strategies. For the first, in an uptrend, when the price had gone rushing upward to distance itself from the 20 bars moving average, but came back to touch it with a smaller volume on that retracement, the hypothesis was disproved when the evidence showed that the trigger candle was not the end of the pull back down. In that case, the stop placed at the bottom of this candle was executed.

For the second, also in an uptrend, the breakout of a strong level of resistance tested several times would allow the anticipation of a strong price advance, continuing in the established direction, the risk being that the price would turn around and return to make a lower low. So, it was the location of the stop since at that level the uptrend, being the instigator condition of the position, was denied.

As for the process anticipating that an upward trend would turn into a bearish reversal, driven by a divergence of indicators and signaled by an inverted hammer (negative candle) or a Gravestone (deadly negative candle), the risk was that the price came back up to make a new high and, therefore, the stop was placed at that level. Thus, the change of direction hypothesis was distorted by the evidence of a reconfirmed uptrend.

In all cases, the stops were an important part of risk management, as they ensured that losses were small. It was an automatic security measure triggered if the price came to touch that level, since the initial hypothesis for the trade proved to be wrong. In fact, Mr. Townsend said often to traders:

"If your reason is out, get out!"

In addition, the calculation of a target also had its place in the risk management.

For example, if the risk of loss was fifty cents on 3,000 shares, it accounted for $1,500 and the target had to have the ability to earn two or three times that amount.

In general, a cheap stock had less potential for gain or loss in dollars, in the same day and for the same amount of shares than another worth more. Obviously, an average 1% movement on a twenty-five dollars stock was a lot less money than 1% on another worth ninety-five dollars. That is why the preparation of the work plan considered very carefully the instrument relative volatility (Beta). The preliminary study was to project a gain several times larger than the possible loss, according to the calculation of the risk represented by the level of the stop location.

I understood that the effectiveness of a trader was measured not only by the performance of the portfolio, but also by a favorable ratio of performance against risks. The bonus or reward was always based on the rate of return (profit) at the end of the year, quarter or month, but the potential for career success was defined by the quality of the results of risk-return.

Therefore, a final figure reporting a gain of 4%, while the risk was 35% (calculated as the percentage difference between the peak and the trough of the account results), was a far worse performance relatively that the appearance implied. Indeed, on a portfolio basis of a million dollars, if gains had propelled the value to one million six hundred thousand (peak) and huge losses had reduced it to a profit of only forty thousand dollars for a total value at the end of the year of one million and forty thousand dollars (trough), the enormous volatility of 35% brought in the actual result, not at 4% but only at 0.114%.

This trader was earning 60% of the fund value and, subsequently, had constantly lost to get a very poor outcome. Undoubtedly, the reason was due to poor risk management and a lack of preparedness.

The Sharpe ratio was a popular measure of evaluation. This quotient measured the profitability of a portfolio of assets compared to a risk-free investment, such as a government bond and this excess was calculated per unit of risk. Its use made it possible to compare the performance of managers with opposing strategies, as well as different risk management. More simply, the Sharpe ratio showed how an investment would pay an investor, with respect to risk.

When the comparison was made based on a common reference data, it was easier to judge since it measured the amount of return adjusted for each level of risk taken. It was calculated by subtracting the risk-free rate from the annualized revenue and dividing the result by the standard deviation of profits. This gauge could be applied across a number of funds with different levels of profitability and volatility, to determine if they generated an alpha (outperformance) by taking on additional risks.

A good Sharpe ratio varied according to the strategy of the fund, but a level above one was considered an attractive return.

Knowing that financial management was part of the trading system that decides the size of the position, the price at which to enter and above all, the percentage of capital exposed, I had to decide on a reasonable degree of risk with respect to potential profits. That's why I spent a large part of my preparation calculating these details, even though my transactions were still only "on paper" (fictitious).

Moreover, apart from the trader's personal psychology, the level of risk was the most critical concept to be resolved as a trader or manager.

"How much should I bet?"

The answer to this question determined the risk and the earnings potential. The ideal was to divide the funds into a number of very small trades, spread over several different investments or products, in order to get multiple opportunities to make money on the whole.

Although, outside the business, traders were sometimes compared to professional gamblers, I was convinced that the two were very dissimilar.

Years ago, my first husband, who had liked to spend time at casinos tables, told me that some gamblers used a system of martingale or of anti-martingale.

The martingale meant the gambler doubled the bet after every loss and thus, on the first gain all losses were recovered. But in reality, this practice could not be effective because the gaming tables imposed maximum limits per bet. Indeed, a loss ten times in a row (fifteen and sixteen times had been seen) was a colossal sum. For example, starting from a set of $10, the tenth bet had to be $20,480 and the eleventh $40,960. It was therefore impossible to recover the money because, generally, the $10 tables had a limit of $1,000!

On the other hand, the anti-martingale adopted by professional gamblers had some followers among traders. It was only to raise the bets when the positions were winning, although with some limitations.

This scheme seemed more valuable, and in fact, it was the principle of the "Turtles", which I had just learnt. My curiosity being well accepted, I did not hesitate to grab every opportunity to ask questions about trading and, that is how I had found out about this system, during a conversation with one of the brokers of the exchange. It was simply a trend following strategy, with entry on the breakout of a new 20 day high (or a new 55 day high), adding to the position as it profited, under certain conditions.

This amazing method earned the youngest of them more than thirty million dollars in four years, so of course, I wanted to get familiar with all the details to apply them myself.

Whether in casinos or in trading, the principle of a good capital operation resulted from calculating the risk accurately and, eventually, from raising the stakes only if the initial position earned enough to cover the risk of the added amount. In addition, it was necessary to move the stops initially placed to new levels of support as the prices kept advancing , and to keep moving the stop up as the price rose in order to stay invested and benefit from the favorable movement to the end, when the stop was finally hit. In a downtrend, the stop was above resistance and the procedure was reversed.

I understood this system and I intended to adopt it.

The great danger was to place too big a bet at the beginning and, even worse, to up the ante if it was losing (average down). Good management was to decide the size of the order, the size of the capital outlay and the ratio of potential gain or performance, measured against the loss or risk.

A stop was simply a precaution to facilitate the management of money.

Relaxation & Pep Talk

Relentless, repetitive self talk is what changes our self-image.

— *Denis Waitley*

With astonishment, I learned that relaxation was part of the trader's preparation and facilitated better risk management.

Stress lessening would allow a reduction in blood pressure as well as heart and respiratory rate decrease, which would result in a general well being. The aim was to avoid losing composure over the unpredictability of the market and so improve performance.

Experience was needed to know how to manage instruments that rattled and indeed, to profit from the volatility which seemed unbearable to novice traders. The nervous tension could easily cause mental exhaustion and was a condition extremely adverse to good performance.

One method used by some people was to write a few words like these:

"I am confident, I control my actions and emotions, I am disciplined, I respect my plan to the letter... etc."

Then, to lie down and relax completely and, once quiet, repeat these motivation phrases. Combining these sentences with pleasant scents, enjoyable sounds and attractive images, all the while imagining a delicious taste, allowed these inspirations to permeate deep into the brain.

By learning to relax and to think positively, it was possible to reach a second state, obtained by the vacuuming of the surroundings.

The subconscious, the part of the brain that directs behavior and habits, was to become available and would allow the hackneyed statements to anchor in the memory, giving rise to a better trader's overall performance. This state of peace made the suggestion easier and this relaxation method aided motivation while facilitating the acquisition of mental health, which was as necessary as physical health.

When a rapid response to a trade was required, the right attitude was then instinctive; hence the importance of this work of relaxation.

The trader's profession required constant psychological effort. In order to strengthen confidence, the trader needed to say optimistic sentences or think positive expressions to enhance self-esteem and to help him become more disciplined, which heightened efficiency.

For example, this kind of self-persuasion led to better risk management if, every day, a phrase was repeated with the affirmation of obedience to prepare and to respect a work plan. Similarly, the habit of expressing encouragements had the advantage of making the trader ready for the trading day and of controlling the emotions, which logically resulted in fewer chances of succumbing to greed or fear, since the brain power was strengthened. With the repetition of these words, the preparation bore more fruit.

It was a sort of "Neuro-Linguistic Programming" (NLP), a method recognized to help master the mind in order to achieve a satisfactory performance. Of course, it was better not to have bad habits in the first place. However, this procedure helped to reprogram the mind, in order to "rewire" the emotional circuits.

I had attended a seminar for people wanting to improve their sales and I had found the information very interesting.

The technique taught applied the principles of neuro-linguistic programming and also used its features. The presenter was a tall, charismatic young man of incredible energy. His name was Anthony Robbins and he was not yet very well known, but I was impressed by his ease in explaining very simply how to overcome failures or phobias, such as the fear of a snake.

When he published a book, I highlighted the most sensitive sentences and asked the children to learn them. But, despite my insistence, I was not very successful in convincing them to be interested and, from time to time I read them a few paragraphs to press on some details I found particularly important.

Undoubtedly, in addition to the study of technical analysis and market behavior, my mental power had to be worked on, in order to improve my psychology, which had to be at its best as well as my physical strength. Indeed, I exercised almost every day, to get a better natural endurance.

However, the sentences of my "Pep-Talk" were not meant to give me a negative assurance. It was not to become arrogant, since there was a big difference between being the best one can be and feeling invincible.

In fact, the disparity was great!

Although sometimes there was a fine enough separation between the two, to be at one's best was positive, while feeling invincible was downright negative and could lead to large errors. In any case, keeping aware of my own behavior and facing the truth was not always easy.

To achieve superior results, the moral efficacy had to be added to the business practice and the necessary experience to perform properly. That was my intention and I was determined to spare no detail to become a great trader.

GREEN LIGHT

Success is doing ordinary things extraordinarily well.

—*Jim Rohn*

At the end of six months, Mr. Townsend said nonchalantly that I was ready.

From now on, I was going to sit at the other end of the table, with the responsibility for managing a one million dollar portfolio. However, if the money was to decline by ten percent, I would have to leave and I would be "thanked" (kicked out).

Out of the earned money at the end of each month, half would be mine and would be transferred within a week to my bank account. No strategy was imposed; the only condition was that the positions would be held for the day only and be closed "before the bell" (which rang at four o'clock, announcing the closing of the New York Stock Exchange).

I could not believe my ears and wanted to jump up and kiss him but I merely smiled, although my eyes were wide and moist from joy.

In a voice trembling with excitement, I thanked him profusely and promised that I would be a good trader, thanks to his training. He seemed amused to see I could not contain my euphoria, and thereupon, I went to take the seat which had been designated to me.

For a moment, I savored the pleasure of having my own post, and thoughtful, I stroked my fingertips on the surface of my new territory.

I felt a mixture of proud achievement with a little anxiety before assuming the challenge. It was up to me to prove that I was up to the task and to reveal that I was as capable of trading as the monsters screaming insults around me. I intended to demonstrate to all that my learning was entrenched in my memory and that my apprenticeship would pay off.

On the trading desk, in front of each post was a computer screen and a low and inclined panel, on which were about one hundred buttons, each corresponding to a "live wire" (direct line) to a broker. Some of these lines were to call a broker located near a specialist on the New York Stock Exchange, according to the "room" where he was located, so as to have immediate access to the station where the stock of interest was exchanged. Other buttons were connected with several brokers in each of the major U.S. investment banks.

A few of the direct lines were to reach "discount brokers" who charged 3 cents per share for their service. The "upstairs brokers" (meaning they were not on the "floor" of the exchange), gave information about the research of their firm and, if the transaction they suggested was really profitable, they could receive up to 10 cents per share in some exceptional cases. However, they were usually paid 6 cents and, on the exit of the trader's position, 8 cents per share for a "good call".

On the wall, a board reserved for research was visible to all. There, every day was compiled a list where the bank issuing the information was indicated by its diminutive (e.g., GS for Goldman Sachs) which was circled and, on the same line a series of symbols were added, followed by several + or - depending on the size of the warning concerning the stocks that had been cited in their morning recommendation.

From the beginning, I had recorded all the "morning calls" and so I had a good idea of the securities to buy or sell. In particular, I had highlighted those made by the most famous analysts, in order to use them later as reference, for the quality of their report.

I was ready, but I decided to give myself a day or two to prepare my trading plan and organize the process of my orders. Also, I had to choose who I preferred to call on the stocks that interested me, because I wanted to be operational from my first day of trading.

The working day ended just after the market closed and every night I had brought back home my little notebook to review what Mr. Townsend had considered important to note. It was full and I knew the contents by heart.

It was also the date of my last class, which began at six p.m. and I had a good hour in front of me, before going to the New York Institute of Finance. I took the opportunity to go to Harry's Bar at the corner of the street, to meet people in the business, as I had been advised to do.

Most men from the floor met there. They all knew each other and were just like family. At the end of their trading day, they usually met over cocktails to relax among themselves. As for me, I insisted to only drink sparkling water but my sobriety did not stop me from always be smiling and I was determined to put my shyness aside to ask relevant questions about the business.

To this end, I courageously introduced myself to those who seemed to have the most experience.

Some did not hesitate to give me advice. Knowing where I had started to work, some warned: "Kid: This is not for the faint of heart…" suggesting this activity was too difficult, especially for a woman.

Among brokers and traders, I also met specialists. These people were members of the exchange and had to maintain a "fair and orderly market" in several different stocks.

It was important to know which room every symbol belonged to, in order to call a trusted broker who had rapid access to the post where it was exchanged. Indeed, the stock could only be bought or sold on the exchange through its appointed specialist.

That evening in Harry's Bar, one of them invited me to the New York Stock Exchange and I was delighted to accept.

NEW YORK STOCK EXCHANGE

*The most important single central fact about a free market
is that no exchange takes place unless both parties benefit.*

—*Milton Friedman*

In the hedge fund, from the opening to the closing of the market, there was no interruption. Each trader ordered his lunch, which was delivered to the desk and swallowed quickly between two telephone calls. However, my boss pushed his traders to meet brokers and specialists to develop friendships. Information and anecdotes exchanged during these get-togethers were often interesting and these conversations resulted in getting an overview of firms' views or opinions.

As long as there were no open positions while leaving the office, anything that could help gain a better performance was encouraged.

That morning I asked my boss' permission and, without hesitation, he allowed me to visit the New York Stock Exchange. Obviously, I preferred to go there before my first trade, to get a better idea of what was happening on the floor.

Dressed in my most elegant suit, I arrived at the New York Stock Exchange, which was only five minutes away from my office. After passing through the security checkpoint and getting back my handbag subjected to metal detectors, I met an assistant who was waiting for me inside to give me a badge. The trading was done in four different rooms, connected to each other on the same level. They were called the Main Room, the Blue Room, the Extended Blue Room and the Garage.

The young man invited me to follow him and told me that we were going to the Blue Room where we would find the specialist he worked for. After climbing some stairs and going through a maze of corridors, he put his badge on the top of a turnstile to get in and I did the same with the badge he had given me.

The room was packed. Most of the men were dressed in the lightweight navy blue broker coat on which was a plate with large three-digits numbers. Some were grouped around different posts and others hurried to walk in all directions. Apparently, they were forbidden to run.

Suddenly the noise stopped.

I saw smiling faces turn towards me and I heard thunderous applause. Quickly, I turned around to see who was the celebrity behind me, but the assistant laughed and, to my surprise, informed me that they had all read the magazine and were waiting for my visit.

Incredulous, I raised my eyebrows. I had not thought about it at all ... However, I hid my surprise behind a smile and shook the hands of most of them. They were respectful and admiring. As for me, I was a little embarrassed.

To talk about something else, I inquired why one of the men had a cross on his shoulder, made with two wide strips of gray tape, and I learned that the sign indicated that he suffered there, so he would not be bumped into.

Each station looked like a big mushroom surrounded by a series of screens and several specialists and their assistants were grouped around it.

Guided by the young assistant, I went across the rooms called the garage and the main room, before arriving at the blue room where stood the post of Mr. Phillips, the specialist who had invited me and who was responsible for six different stocks.

After greeting me and introducing the people around him, he showed me his order-book, giving me some explanation on the routing of the trades and on their execution process. Unlike the majority of brokers, he did not wear a navy coat, though he too, exhibited a numbered plaque on his jacket.

His suit was well cut and I noticed that all the specialists were very elegantly dressed.

His mission was to balance the market and, to do that, he was responsible for buying shares if too many orders came to be sold and if investors panicked. Also, he had to sell shares as well, if too many buyers were rushing to get in. In addition, he took positions for his firm and had a result of gains or losses at the end of the day, like any other trader. I did not doubt for a second that he was excellent and probably one of the best, since few people could know better than him the behavior of the stocks he made the market of.

His explanations were given quite affably and they seemed perfectly logical and clear. With appreciation, I thanked him and his assistant before leaving the exchange.

With this visit, I had acquired a vision of the route taken after an order had been given to the broker, or when a trader called for a "look" before or after taking a position. The order was made by phone and the broker moved physically to pass it on to the specialist. Thereupon, the requested information or the order execution was communicated to the broker, who reported it by calling back the trader.

All this took but a few seconds. It was important to choose a trusted broker, who could easily have access to the specialist in charge of the stock traded, to save time.

I was a little anxious to start, even if I had eagerly waited for this moment. I had high hopes to be up to what was expected of me and I did not want to disappoint Mr. Townsend, who had given me a chance I would probably never have had without him.

Back at the office, I decided to watch the behavior of some securities without taking position and I spent part of the afternoon organizing my screen.

I set up my graphics so that they would automatically have the tools most relevant to me, in order to be better prepared to start working. Also, I analyzed several stocks and I took note of those which acted remarkably well or badly, compared to the overall market or to the behavior of their sector, to prepare for trading them the next day.

Very advanced mathematical studies and analysis skills could not supplant careful preparation and strict discipline. I had decided to commit to this behavior, knowing what was important to me personally, how far I wanted to go and why.

To start, I had to be at my best.

My classes at the New York Institute of Finance had finished the previous day and despite all my significant knowledge of analysis, I adopted the method "KISS" (Keep It Simple, Stupid) which, in other words, meant not to complicate things.

In fact, the more added tools there were on a graph, the more its perspective was blurred.

On my platform, I kept the charts with only my candles and several moving averages, the volume, two indicators of trend confirmation and another to verify its strength. Then, on the quotes list, I entered all the symbols in the same order as Mr. Townsend had placed them on his screen, with the indexes which gave indications of the breadth and the volatility of the market first, followed by a number of securities grouped together by industry, to be able to look at them simultaneously and to see how they correlated with other sectors of activity.

Trader

FIRST TRADE

*Trust yourself. Create the kind of self that you will be happy
to live with all your life. Make the most of yourself by fanning
the tiny, inner sparks of possibility into flames of achievement.*

— *Golda Meir*

Early the next morning, the mild anxiety of the day before gave
way to the excitement of proving my abilities. My morale was high
and I was anticipating a good day.

Even though I still had a lot to discover, I was finally going to
practice and use what I had learned. These few months on the desk
had clearly shown me that being a good trader did not happen by
luck. It was a job.

Following an excellent education, the best way to gain experience
was to trade with money and not anymore "on paper." I had worked
hard during my six months of trading in the "virtual world", but now
it was for real! Now, I was going to be judged on my skills and proper
use of my training.

An image of a jungle came to the forefront of my mind. Yes, this
profession was best defined as a jungle. I accepted it and was aware
of the dangers.

I was surrounded by beasts with insatiable needs, who, hungry for
blood, did not hesitate to attack any prey in their path. My attitude
was different although I had to impose myself among these traders.

Around me, it was kill or be killed, but I knew that it would be
possible for me to prove I belonged there, by being well prepared and

disciplined. I had to survive in the midst of the jungle, among these fearsome creatures who saw me as a nuisance or as a competition to be eliminated.

A woman assistant was an inconvenient but sometimes necessary intrusion, but a female trader was out of the question. Geez, I had to be on my guard, do my job accurately and adopt a foolproof risk management.

I was ready for action.

That first day, upon my arrival at 7:30 am, I conducted my usual short overview of what was happening in the world. I looked for the political and economic news, and the information that could influence the stock market trend.

In general, the exchanges in other continents were somewhat up that day. The SP futures (the 500 largest companies in the United States, whose shares were compiled by Standard & Poors) were slightly higher too, in "pre-market" (before the opening).

The "index futures" gave the "temperature" of the mood that would prevail during the day and were a good indication. I also, as a matter of daily routine, consulted the economic calendar because, of course, everything could change if governmental figures or quarterly reports of some large companies were announced.

For almost all the traders on the desk, it was better to wait until the reports were out, instead of taking unnecessary risks by being positioned beforehand. In fact, professionals had a bias towards probabilities and reacted to the results according to their individual differences, unlike the consensus found among analysts.

It was not a casino. Red or black, negative or positive, they benefited, following the trend and the flow of money. They had experience in understanding the economic data and were making trading decisions on them. As for me, I was not yet ready to act or react on these.

To start I had the intention of doing nothing complicated and to use only what I fully understood. I had prepared my plan, supported by my graphs, and I was determined to be content with my research.

The goal was undoubtedly to win, but the priority was first to survive. Anything was possible and numerous opportunities were present to grasp, as long as I was part of that game; outside, they were useless.

During my training, I had entered fictitious transactions that had all been winners ... However, my first "real life" trade was not.

Before I even started to work on what I had prepared, a broker called me from the floor. He had often contacted my colleagues and they trusted him so, very innocently, I thought he was doing me a favor...

He whispered:

"Someone is working an order to purchase one million shares of IBM (International Business Machines). There are just ten thousand offered. Buy them now, but call another broker and be discreet... I'm sure you'll make at least two points."

I thought, twenty thousand dollars profit ... Not a bad start!

Immediately, I pushed a button for another "three cents broker" (a broker paid 3 cents per share) and bought 10000 IBM "at the market" (on the offer).

I imagined making money easily and I smiled.

Immediately, I wrote in the margins of my journal to give him my exit order and to pay him a large commission. I had to act quickly not to allow another buyer the time to take hold of the shares at this price before me. Once the position was entered, and as a precaution, I decided to consult the recent analysts' reports.

Slightly puzzling, as I could not find anything particularly brilliant.

I followed the quote closely, as I had seen Mr. Townsend do so many times, and I noticed the transactions made on the offer compared to those made on the bid. It was obvious that if a large buyer was eager to grab the shares quickly, he would do so at the offer price, just like I did. If he had plenty of time, he would bid lower, instead.

But nobody seemed in any rush to buy...

I frowned and studied the chart. What I saw was not reassuring. Technically, there was a strong resistance a few points higher and the only truly solid, major support was not visible until thirty points lower, around $100, well below what I had paid.

Should I wait until the buyer showed his nose?

I could not imagine any other reason for this broker call than a welcome gesture to try to be among those with whom I was going to work regularly. He had a good reputation, was esteemed by other traders ... How could I doubt his good intentions?

I had felt so confident of profiting the way I had always done in my "paper trades" that I had not asked any questions. Without even checking, I had blindly believed him and had placed an order totaling over one million three hundred thousand dollars, using my account leverage, which allowed me positions up to two million.

The more I looked at IBM activity the more I noted that a minimal number of trades were being made on an uptick (the offer price by a buyer). With horror, I realized that I had probably made a serious mistake.

I was getting very scared and I felt my stomach tighten. Worse, I did not have a stop and I saw no indication to anticipate a rebound in prices, before four points at best.

I tried to breathe deeply and not lose my cool but, gradually, I realized that all my good intentions not to be trapped were damned. All my promises to do what I had learned and to be disciplined had fallen to pieces and I had ignored the warnings, in my very first minutes of work.

I fought against feelings of panic, the most dangerous emotion a trader can have.

The quote continued to show 90% downticks (sales) and I tried to accept the idea that maybe I should get out of this position. I did not want to make the most common mistake, which was to keep a bad trade, hoping the price would come back. Should there be a loss, I had to take it without shame and, above all, avoid aggravating the situation.

I had to try to think straight. Was it really possible that the broker had deliberately tricked me? Surely not! So before reacting too impulsively, I called back the other broker whom I had chosen to buy IBM and asked him for a "look" (who bought – more exactly, through which bank, who sold and how much).

A fundamental rule was to get out of a position that went wrong, but I would have been sick to my stomach to do so and exit without a "look", giving me a more detailed account of the situation, not visible on my screen. This service justified the preference of a person on the floor. With fifty cents loss now on the price, the broker gave me his report:

"Vendors for most, the few buyers were for only 100 or 200 shares. Apparently, a broker worked a huge amount for sale. Well, nothing else."

A shiver of fear went through me like an electric shock.

I had acted on the recommendation of a broker who regularly called traders of the table. What if it was to win at my expense?

It was then that I remembered:

"If your reason is out, get out!"

My reason for entering was certainly gone.

Without any hesitation, I gave him the order to sell immediately my ten thousand IBM shares "at the market!"

At least the maxim "Get out" had saved me from waiting and hanging on.

Anxious and uncomfortable, throat tight, I threw a glance across at Mr. Townsend. He seemed indifferent, but I was sure he had not missed a word.

To get to the bottom of this, even if I had no position any longer, I called the broker who had recommended the purchase.

He answered evasively that vendors had appeared and he knew nothing more; he was sorry. I hung up the phone without further comment, to answer the call of the broker who had bought and sold for me. He gave me the average of the execution prices.

Although my decision had been quick, my loss was very large since there were very few buyers. My market order had collapsed all small bids, one underneath the other, and I guess the specialist did a good job, not to let the price plummet too fast.

My eyes looked at the faces of the traders around the table. I was convinced that one of them had offered the ten thousand shares for sale, asking the broker to tell me to buy them, in order to have the necessary short sale uptick. Indeed, with shares, one could not sell short without the trade execution being done at a higher price than the last (uptick). It was a law to avoid prices going down too quickly.

So, it had not been a buyer for a million shares... This was a seller...of that, I was certain.

Only a novice would have been stupid enough to take the offer the way I did. My loss was nearly ten thousand dollars, which the trader had probably made at my expense and all this, in less than ten minutes.

I had difficulty swallowing, my hands were shaking a little and, although I apparently kept my composure to the outside world, I felt terribly hurt.

Naturally, I did not want a scandal...but it was a crime.

With great effort, I forced myself to stand up straight and give no appearance of anything wrong, although my legs were shaky and I felt bruised all over. I walked to the ladies room, splashed my face with cold water and did some deep breathing to relax.

Of course, this was the perfect time to show I could get hit and still stand up. I had chosen this fight, entered the jungle, and now, I had to accept the attacks and the cheap shots, as well as the victories. I had to prove I was not an easy prey and not defeated!

Going back to my place, I still intended to say aloud for the whole desk to hear:

"Thanks for the lesson!"

However, I decided to keep these words to myself and I sat down in what I hoped was a dignified silence, knowing that it would be pointless to make any comment.

A few minutes later, the IBM price was two points lower. At least I had had the strength to get out quickly as obviously this trap could have cost me much more.

At the end of the day, the shares were down three points, recovering slightly from a four points loss in the course of the trading session.

Good Resolutions

*Always bear in mind that your own resolution
to succeed is more important than any other.*

—*Abraham Lincoln*

Even after this unpromising start, the day was just beginning. It was barely ten o'clock in the morning and I still had several hours to trade the way I had prepared, without allowing myself to become obsessed with the lesson I just learned.

Like a boxer after a first painful blow, I had strength in reserve, I was not confused and above all, I had not lost confidence.

With determination, I wiped from my mind all traces of this experience and began to work with my research and the graphs I had prepared the day before. I began to buy shares that looked to be the strongest and I sold short in larger number the weakest, since just at that time, the market had begun to rollover, losing the advance of the first few minutes.

I also wrote down the symbols of the stocks that, despite the early morning rise in their sector of activity, had opened down and I sold some of them which fitted my conditions. Knowing that the others would have a more pronounced weakness if the general market went down further, I kept my little list to the side, with the intention to sell them "short" when I found the time to study them more closely.

Certainly, IBM was one of them!

As the morning advanced I grew calmer. I had now returned to trading in the way I had practiced "on paper" throughout all these months of preparation.

All my trades were limited to 2000 shares and I stayed with graphs of five minutes intervals. The studies I had prepared so carefully showed me at which price to enter and exit with the least possible risk, looking for a profit, small indeed, but still a profit.

My intention was to make money on the total number, not on each of my trades in particular. I knew that the key to success was to win small, repeatedly and consistently, and therefore, I applied myself to it.

Out of all my technical analysis, I chose to look first for the velocity at which a price had evolved, especially if the movement was accompanied by a higher volume of transactions than usual. Although it was one of the simplest and easiest indications to notice, it was one that seemed to predict the next movement with the most efficiency.

After a strong advance in an uptrend, the indication was to wait for the price to go back in the opposite direction, which retraced part of the progression with a decreased volume, until it reached and touched its 20 periods moving average.

I watched carefully for the trigger to the trade, a candle now in the direction of the established trend while many of my other tools indicated approval of the same price. I placed my entry at that level and positioned my stop on the order book, as soon as I got the report of my execution price, just below the beginning of the initial move. If the stop was hit, it was proof that the regression was not completed or that the trend had changed course, which meant my trade no longer had potential. But I had guarded against a large loss.

For example, when the indices rolled over and started to show a downtrend, I looked for a stock quickly losing fifty cents (high velocity), and getting away from its average (MA20) with a huge volume (2 or 3 times normal size), to place my order as soon as the price retraced upward to touch the moving average again, with a reduced volume on its way back.

The end of this upward movement, often accounted for half or two-thirds of the initial decline and was signaled by a small negative candle (a doji or an inverted hammer). My stop was at the point where the price would have turned positive on the day, or exceeding the signal candle.

I bought stocks that were up (green) and sold short those down (red). Moreover, at any time, I had a sort of balance between sales and purchases, my short positions being in a bigger number, since the market was now bearish.

On the one hand, my short positions were stocks acting really badly and, on the other, my few longs were symbols showing strength and ignoring the overall market poor behavior, while attracting most buyers' interest.

This style suited me. At least, I depended only on myself.

Without interruption on that first day, I traded a lot of stocks, some of them several times. After booking a profit, I waited for a digestive wave to retrace part of the move, to re-enter.

I was working steadily and to my great pleasure could feel the rhythm of the market. My activity was so intense that I did not have the time to think about my earlier misfortune.

I even forgot to eat lunch.

On the wall, hung eight round clocks with different times. Below each was the name of the city whose time they displayed. New York was just in front of me and at 3:55 p.m., I gave orders to close all my positions.

At the end of the day, I had recuperated 60% of my losses. My P & L (Profit & Loss) was still negative, but provided I was really vigilant, I knew I could turn positive within a few days at most. Ultimately, I realized that I had learned something very important:

Never act on a tip, never!

After the close, I was not disappointed with my attitude and I wrote that in my journal.

I felt I had what it took to succeed, if I did not do anything stupid. Curiously, I had regained my composure and I had shown a mental strength that surprised me. However, my account was still losing and was nearly four thousand dollars lower for the day.

With the intention of learning to do more of what was good and, therefore, get to make fewer mistakes, I was determined to write down as many details as possible after each day, to thoroughly immerse myself in every circumstance I had experienced.

I now decided also to memorize all the sayings of the business, realizing that Mr. Townsend's little phrase, "If your reason is out, get out," coming back to my mind, had saved me.

And then, another expression had helped me all day:

"The trend is your friend." Following the trend, I had won. I had to continue on this path, and not forget to note all of my transactions' details. The aim was to highlight what was profitable and also to mention what was not, to avoid it in the future.

That evening, I visited the men from the floor in their favorite hangout, a detour that seemed necessary since it would allow me to be part of their clan.

I asked one of the older traders what was the worst misfortune that could happen after entering a position. He replied with a smile:

"I can tell you a scenario that has happened hundreds of times. It is always the same, when one is too stubborn!"

Immediately, I thought being stubborn was indeed one of my bad qualities.

He told me a terrible story.

DRAMATIC SCENARIO

The ode lives upon the ideal, the epic upon the grandiose, the drama upon the real.

—*Victor Hugo*

It was a day like any other.

Only, for some reason, the trader had not prepared his plan in advance. Whether acting on a tip or a seemingly solid research, he had entered a large transaction without having a stop placed mentally or on the book. Obviously, without having worked out his maximum loss limit in advance, he knew the dangers were multiplied, but he felt very confident and he had no doubt. His information was solid, or at least he thought so.

At first, his trade was doing well and it earned quickly. The behavior of the value strengthened his conviction and, indeed, he was a little angry at not having invested more, while he looked forward to his gains.

A few hours later these profits had disappeared and his position moved into negative. He had not studied in advance the strategic price levels, and so was not prepared for the unexpected. He could only pray that this price reduction was a temporary setback...

No matter, because he was sure to be right!

When his losses grew to a point where the cost was seriously troubling, he remained convinced that this unexpected move was only temporary. He had bought in and therefore, persuaded himself that the trade was surely going to move in his direction. The price was likely to return; it must return, to prove that his reasoning (or information) was right.

Anyway, he was determined to cling to his trade and resolute that it would come right in the end.

Mentally, he had assumed a stop level so ridiculously low that it would be quite impossible to touch, and then, when the price approached it, he had rejected the idea and concluded that it was necessary to leave more room for the position to "breathe".

The price continued to drop and was now well below his first stop level.

Desperately, he called around to see what the problem was, without receiving any tangible or reassuring answer. Nobody could comfort him with anything positive.

He persisted anyway...

But the minutes passed and nothing got better. Hope turned into frustration and the worse things grew, the more fear began to settle.

When a kind of consolidation seemed to appear on the graph, this gave him confidence, but suddenly, the value collapsed again.

With his eyes on the ever plunging price approaching an extremely low level, the trader felt his strength weakening, in tandem with the value.

He was unable to think logically.

To regain his senses and relax, he went out to smoke a cigarette and drink a coffee. Of course if he left the screen for a bit, things were bound to improve... However, upon his return to his desk, a shock awaited him!

While he had thought that a good level of support was evident on the graph, and the price could not get worse, the stock was now in freefall.

Seized with anger and panic, he reacted in the worst possible way. He doubled his position to reduce his average cost, while exposing his capital dangerously. But, contrary to his belief that the value could not go any lower, it sank inexorably and tumbled into the abyss, without mercy.

With the leverage he was using, his account was now decreased by half. He was in the dangerous mindset of feeling he had no choice but to try to chase the loss. If he sold now it would crystallize the loss, he thought. Far better, he told himself, to hang on in there.

He simply could not imagine there was still time to get out and avoid the consequences that he would surely regret all his life. Instead of giving up with his account so severely depleted, he gambled his career.

When the stock finally appeared to stabilize, he boldly added to the size of his bet, convinced more than ever that the rise in price was imminent and would soon enable him to make up his losses. He persuaded himself that this had to be true. Since his average was reduced even more, although at the cost of a huge capital contribution, he was caught in a mesh and could not admit defeat.

He could not believe this was happening. From the start of his career he had never had such an experience. Until now, he had always been lucky and he still convinced himself he would surely laugh later, if only he could survive this unfortunate turn of events.

Finally, the price appeared to climb a few cents, though a little too slowly in his view. Well, that was that ... Then suddenly, the price continued its precipitous descend, yet again.

Frozen, like a deer caught in the headlights and overwhelmed by panic, he was paralyzed, queasy, badly wanting to vomit and feeling sick.

His face was deathly pale when he felt a tap on his shoulder and heard his manager's voice, snarling with rage

"You have a 'margin call' and if you don't close this transaction immediately, we will do it for you!"

Trembling, the unfortunate picked up the phone to whisper his order, in a broken voice:

"Sell at the market! Just hit the bid..." (Without working the order, on the bid).

End of story.

The career of this obstinate was over. This was the best way to lose a fortune and to bury a trader's job.

As the narrative unfolded, I imagined living the scene and seeing myself among the many traders who were forced to leave the profession after a similar adventure.

Not having a stop on a trade (mental or on the book), and sticking to that stop, engendered losses as huge as unexpected, caused above all by the tenacious behavior of a stubborn trader.

Just yesterday, this story would have seemed exaggerated, but with my recent experience and my morning troubles, I could easily understand how such a disaster could happen without warning ...

The story showed me what could have been the end of my own career, which would have lasted only one day. If I had not been the careful student of Mr. Townsend and if my mindset had been rigid, I would not have got out as quickly as I did.

I would have suffered large capital losses and probably psychological ruin as well.

That would have been a tragedy!

I vowed inwardly to work on myself to not be stubborn. Clearly, this was an extremely dangerous fault in my new job.

One thing was certain, this catastrophe could have happened to me with my first trade of ten thousand shares. I thought with relief that, fortunately, discipline was mandatory on my trading desk. It was one of the first things I had learned.

My six months alongside Mr. Townsend had probably saved me from hanging on to a losing trade.

After thanking the broker I went home, promising myself never to forget this story.[2]

---

2 Several years later, with increased leverage on futures, billions were lost by young traders who experienced the same scenario.

Self-Control

*Self-control is the chief element in self-respect,
and self-respect is the chief element in courage.*

— *Thucydides*

The majority of errors on the trading floor were caused by loss of control, a problem affecting especially the "rookies" (beginners).

When a trader was "thanked" and lost his job, the case was often related, one way or another, to a lack of self-control. The surrender to emotions caused destructive actions, taken while the trader was unable to respond to unexpected events in a calm, considered and intelligent way.

Since it was established that the brain's ability regressed as a result of stress or fear, it was essential to adopt a system of preparation to avoid reaching that point. This ensured the longevity of the trader in his career, a profession that, with time and experience, was one of the most profitable businesses in the world.

Self-control meant having self-knowledge. For this, it was necessary for the trader to question his own motivation, to determine his life's priorities, to define what were the most important things for him and to be familiar with the feelings that most deeply affected his mind. He had to take into account his specific character traits and, if he was proud of one of them, use it to express his dearest wishes, in order to be more motivated.

Determined to have everything on my side, I asked my family and friends how they interpreted my character and how they perceived my priorities. Then I noted their responses to decipher what defined me.

REMINISCENCES OF A WALL STREET TRADER

The same features were often mentioned. Apparently, I was generous, fair, committed, hardworking, pragmatic and stubborn. With this information, I could combine my human values with my job and express some sentences of encouragement to define my goal. I could then write this expression at the end of the trading day and read it the next day for moral support.

For example, if I chose the value of being generous, the conclusion of my activities would include this goal:

"By being disciplined and following my plan, my work will be rewarded with profits, allowing me to be generous with my family."

Also, to acquire good self-control, I had to rigorously respect the essential measures to attain success and for that, I wrote down small reminders:

- ✓ Keep a journal. Reserve a time in the evening to note the details of the trading day, and remain objective in the analysis of positive activities as well as the maneuvers in need of improvement. Thereupon, make a promise to do better.

- ✓ Have no order or position in place just before the announcement of significant news, the price often reacts like a whip lash, resulting in casualties on either side. Wait half an hour for the surprise to settle.

- ✓ Early in my career, I should not take a position if the markets are extremely volatile and turbulent. This avoids many problems.

- ✓ Consider my shortfalls, not as failures, but as encouragement to follow my plan. Also, get out of half the trade at breakeven and take profits early. "Nobody gets poor by taking profits, as early as they may be."

- ✓ Never act on advice blindly, without studying the facts. There are as many chances of losing as winning. Moreover, I should decide myself the reasons to enter. Any information received might not be interpreted correctly and the outcome would be a gamble.

✓ Go step by step to advance in my career, without trying to skip the necessary stages to acquire knowledge and experience.

✓ Once a trade is a cause of anxiety, get out immediately.

✓ Cultivate my mind. It is especially important to avoid feeling invincible because some transactions were good or to fall into a state of depression because some of them are losing, which is an unhealthy attitude. Any trader should consider his work as a business; it is not a matter of luck. I must stay positive and do the job, accepting that losses as well as profits are an integral part of the occupation.

✓ Respect money. The trader honors his work as much as himself, by following his plan and staying disciplined. It results in a deserved success, which shows that money is respected as an important tool.

My self-control could prevent me from making mistakes and allow me to be effective, a necessity all the more important since my expenses were growing rapidly. I enrolled my kids to join sports activities, which were a strain on my budget but seemed essential to their development, while getting involved in an athletic activity they enjoyed.

Thierry chose tennis and Maxime was just the right age to start karate.

Thus, the additional cost beyond their school tuition was a pressure that added to the previous ones. I had to be especially disciplined to do my job and start bringing in profits. Since earnings were paid at the beginning of the following month, the money I would make in the next few weeks would enable me to meet these new obligations.

My Journal

The evening of my first day as a trader, I wrote the details of my positions, with the mention of how my performance could have been better and the event that all could have been worse. In retrospect, if I had not followed the floor broker, I would have won $6,000 on my first day. On the other hand, if I had bought more shares at each loss of a point, (a method called "averaging down") so that my average cost was lower, my losses would have been greatly increased.

Enlarging a losing trade, for a lower average purchase price, was prohibited on the desk. Otherwise, if I had made this mistake, it would have cornered me and prevented from doing any other transactions… not to mention that it would probably have cost me fifty thousand dollars.

These notes were going to help me keep track of all my decisions in relation to events. If I won, I wanted to know why and how and if I lost, I needed to analyze all the circumstances that led my preparation or my execution to not being as successful as expected.

My "log board" was divided into three parts, per trade and per day. The first was reserved for the lessons and encouragement of the day previous, the second observed the entry price of each trade with the stop, initial target and result and the third was a general comment on my activities, with a mention of what I had done well.

The latter was copied on the page that would begin the next day. Therefore every morning I started the execution of my trading plan with encouraging statements.

Then I stuck my list of good intentions on a rigid sheet of paper, which would serve as my diary's guard page, to consult daily.

In the first line, I wrote in large letters what I had promised myself that morning:

"Do not listen to tips... Never. Ever!"

Moreover, it appeared in red as if I used my blood for ink.

By using my previous weaknesses to gain the necessary strength and experience for the next day, my journal was considering what I had done well, highlighted the reason for the discrepancy or clumsiness made in relation to the execution of my plan and emphasized the right way to proceed, while remaining overall positive with a comforting remark.

The trader's profession was a continuous learning process and if I was mindful as to what was done wrong and what could be improved, I could move towards a better performance.

This booklet would be my shield against the enemy known to sleep inside each trader. It would prevent the negative influence expressed by emotions, while helping me to be better prepared and therefore more disciplined. It also served to define what were the times when I was most successful, to assess the method behind my transactions and the effectiveness of my strategies, without neglecting to assess the value of my analysis.

The particular advantage of including all situations, good and bad, was to be able to check them regularly and to relive the circumstances, to anchor all the lessons learned in my mind.

Without it, I could forget, deliberately or not, some details that would have been too depressing...

And I did not intend to see them renewed!

To do this, from my early days as a trader, a transaction was not complete, even though it had been exited, without being registered in my journal with the details to remember.

If I did not follow the procedures of my trading plan properly or if the interpretation of my technical analysis indicators was bad, I would obviously lose money. But what would cost me even more was not trying to learn from past mistakes, to avoid repeating them in the future.

This log board was both my travel companion and my compass too.

After expressing my findings, this report allowed me to prepare all the better my future trades.

The job was a balance between knowledge and psychology. Being intimately connected with my analysis, I would win in reflection time and gradually eliminate the emotions that could have prevented me from being at the top of my ability.

I also realized that taking smaller positions suited me better and I was much more comfortable with two or three thousand shares than with ten thousand, a size requiring both more liquidity (more orders purchase / sale to have an immediate execution) and volume (larger transactions).

On the guard page, below my list of promises, I wrote my daily goal and circled it in red:

"Earn $2000 per day and minimize risk through preparation as well as perfect discipline."

The lesson of my first trading day showed that trades with greatly reduced size had generated profits, unlike the ten thousand shares traded without a plan, which had resulted in a significant loss.

MODUS OPERANDI

*Decide what you want, decide what you are willing
to exchange for it. Establish your priorities and go to work.*

—H. L. Hunt

The night after my first trades, I could not sleep.

Instead of staying in bed, I felt the need to write all the qualifications I should possess for success and performance. This list would be added to my first rule to never negotiate on a tip.

Thus, I immersed myself in what I had learned and listed everything I promised to do:

- ✓ Acquire all necessary knowledge and take additional courses to complete the education required to excel in trading.

- ✓ Do not think I know everything without studying and do not believe in a magic system (or martingale) to make a fortune. This is to avoid a rude awakening to reality.

- ✓ Do not try to take shortcuts and do homework and preparation.

- ✓ Know that beginner's instinct is rarely the right reaction.

- ✓ Know the tools and how to use them with expertise.

- ✓ Be disciplined, go to work wholeheartedly and have a strong ambition to succeed.

- ✓ Have a strategy.

✓ Use a trading plan.

✓ Develop an excellent risk management.

✓ Have a perfect understanding and interpretation of technical analysis. This study represents an asset and an advantage over the competition. By using it in a daredevil environment, it helps to decide quickly and to understand prices reactions in seconds.

✓ Act with courage, determination and the will to succeed.

✓ Have a positive attitude, be cool and in possession of all faculties.

✓ Conquer impatience, wait for the opportunities and know how to recognize them.

✓ Do not rush into a trade without thinking; instead follow a plan.

✓ Accept that nothing is 100% guaranteed.

✓ Demonstrate a positive and responsible attitude, whether win or lose.

✓ Trade according to personal style not that of others, but learn from the example of the great masters.

✓ Stay positive and follow the direction of the trend, but know how to recognize a reversal. "The trend is your friend."

✓ Consider trading as a business to run.

✓ Set goals to target and be profitable.

✓ Work hard every day and prepare an action plan, with care and precision, to act confidently and without hesitation.

✓ Be honest to self and to others.

✓ Be determined, motivated and hang on. Accept that success does not happen overnight and commit the energy to stay ahead of fierce competition.

✓ Adopt trading as a profession and not a casino game.

✓ Love my job. Performing passion never gives the impression of working and becomes exciting and enriching as well, in every way. Novelty is constantly there and profitable choices abound; the key is simply to know how to sort them.

✓ Understand the psychology of the masses and know that the study of its development is as important as basic research and economics.

✓ Follow the rules of the trade, while acquiring better knowledge day by day.

✓ Study others' common mistakes to benefit from their experience and make sure not to repeat them.

✓ Develop patience. Accept that a position is not always profitable immediately, but become very impatient if the trade is losing.

✓ Do not be afraid to lose, but act immediately to limit the damage. Do not stay in a trade proving wrong.

✓ Be aware of risk at any time.

✓ Avoid taking too many positions, focus on only a few, without exposing too much capital.

✓ Don't be stubborn. Accept being wrong early and know that any trader can be as often wrong as right. The key is in risk management, as Sir John Maynard Keynes remarked: "Being wrong sometimes is not harmful - especially if you notice it quickly."

✓ Conquer emotions and understand personal psychological reactions.

✓ Stick to a studied risk-return ratio.

✓ Adapt quickly to change. Reduce risk and have stops.

✓ While only raising the stakes on winning positions, remain on guard and consider the possibility that a market may turn suddenly and without warning.

- ✓ Trade with discipline, keep my clarity of mind and keep sight of my target successfully.

- ✓ Stay objective, without preconception or prejudice, and do not hesitate to change my position if the market indicates it.

- ✓ Keep my composure. Know that any emotion (hope, shame, greed) proves to be the precursor of losses.

- ✓ Know how to adapt to change. Another phrase of John Maynard Keynes perfectly captures this detail: "When the facts change, I change my mind. What do you do, Sir?"

- ✓ Quickly identify common pitfalls and face them with real solutions.

- ✓ Do not "hope" but stick to the studied plan.

- ✓ Develop practice to trade efficiently. Learn the lesson of every day to gain experience. This will not only pay handsomely, but be rewarded by a deserved respect from all.

- ✓ When in doubt, cut the position and especially, do not view this as a loss but as an opportunity to make another trade with better profit potential.

- ✓ Do not fall asleep on winnings and re-evaluate positions regularly.

- ✓ Keep a log of all activities.

- ✓ Do not blame anything or anyone for losses, mistakes or adverse market conditions. Whatever happens, be responsible.

- ✓ Take profits regularly, even small.

- ✓ Know that a losing position is a message from the market, alerting me to get out. "A bad trade is like a dead fish; the more you keep it, the more it stinks." Good traders do not add up to a bad position, they get rid of it. With a winning position, the market confirms the trader is right.

✓ Write down, after each transaction, the lesson to remember.

✓ Never brag about profits.

✓ Lose an opinion, rather than money.

✓ Do not hesitate to learn; every day brings new awareness.

A very long list, which I decided to know by heart in order to apply it without thinking, since my good habits would become instinctive. Being constantly on the lookout to expand my knowledge, I knew that it was equally as important to tame my emotional reactions and improve my attitude as to apply each lesson perfectly.

With my promises, I went to the office the next day and I followed my plan to the letter. Profits added up to about $4000, so my account turned positive, if only by a few dollars. The joy of not having a deficit in just twenty-four hours strengthened my commitment to have a disciplined behavior, even more.

I was on the right track.

After 4:30 p.m., the trading room was deserted and, since I had a good hour before picking up the kids at school, I took the opportunity to go to Harry's.

There, I met a few people from the "back office" who normally worked later, but took a few minutes break for coffee. I asked the regulars to explain to me the path that transactions took to be honored by their payment and, at the same time, be delivered smoothly. I was interested in knowing the progress of what was happening behind the scenes once the trade was executed, and wanted to familiarize myself to the details.

Of course, I also hung around with other traders and I favored those who showed a lot of experience. Luckily, at the end of a trading day, they were all willing to exchange their anecdotes and, listening to their many stories was always extremely informative.

Sometimes an innocuous little phrase gave me a clue about what I should look for or investigate to acquire additional knowledge.

I understood that it was equally important to know how to "pull the trigger" at the right time to get into a trade and to draw even faster and without hesitation, to get out. The indecision and the hope, waiting for the price to return to an acceptable level was a risk, and was detrimental to the capital as well as the tenure inside this profession.

Keeping a stock not acting as expected caused stress, occupied the mind and prevented you from entering into other transactions of merit for profit.

This statement was unanimous.

THE THREE PILLARS

Seeing much, suffering much, and studying much, are the three pillars of learning.

—*Benjamin Disraeli*

Unlike any other enterprise, trading proved to be a particular world where beginners' instinct was hurtful to their survival. Their willingness to fight to defend their position was a negative behavior.

On the contrary, it was better just to go with the market flow and accept its law.

Managing the business was also different, since trading was characterized by the lack of time available to make decisions, while many were unexpected. This singularity caused a fear response, which could occasionally lead to paralysis of thought. However, the common point between trading work and affairs in general was that success was defined by the achievement of predetermined objectives and, for that particular reason, good preparation was vital.

Physical health counted too. Not having slept the night before was a danger to the trading day, and in that case, it was advised to stay home and recover. Being angry, worried, distracted or worse, being "out of sorts" because of a "hangover" made every transaction a new chance for the trader to "lose his shirt."

Naturally, Mr. Townsend was adamant about it and when he saw a face a little gray, he pointed his finger at it, saying:

"Go home!"

Feeling fit and ready was particularly critical, morally and physically.

A specialist once told me that since he had started working on the New York Stock Exchange, at the beginning of each day, he thought of a phrase that motivated him and reminded him of a trade with very large profits, to get into the right mental attitude, from the start.

I thought it would be helpful to have an intimate slogan to inspire me while helping me to get in the winning mood, but I had not yet found one.

Later, another friend of mine also confided that he sang the theme song of the movie "Rocky" as he stepped onto the floor like a winning boxer, hopping with fists to the sky. It might not have seemed much, but it was his motto and he had a reputation for being a great oil trader on the NYMEX.

To do this job, it was imperative to have a quick mind, a good level of technical analysis, an ease to find and accumulate probabilities (in the strategies), and to have consistency in preparing a meticulous action plan. In addition, to possess the psychology of a winner, it was essential to be able to control emotions and reflexes, while keeping a good composure.

Thus, the stacking up of many probabilities (Preparation and Strategy), the improvement of a better risk-return (Risk Management) and the mental strength to execute the plan with precision and without emotion (Psychological Strength and Discipline) were found to be three pillars supporting an activity as dangerous as profitable.

I was convinced that this business could not stand without these supporting legs, which together should be innate. But, obviously, the main condition for success was simply to comply especially with the money management rules, which determined the position size and the risk exposure.

Also, I had to concentrate to gain a foolproof mental might, in addition to getting good research, preparing my work and perfecting the execution of my trading. Only this behavior would be rewarded.

This extra power would replace the gaps of my lack of experience with a good attitude, to help me achieve more frequent gains while minimizing the problems.

The key unlocking the door to a bright future was to become an accomplished person with the common sense to assemble all the privileges of a comprehensive learning and growth development. This was done through analysis, identification, quantification, implementation, strategy and the monitoring of all. Having a good understanding of myself, using a well-defined plan to accomplish my task and adopting a very healthy and disciplined lifestyle were the necessary conditions leading to success.

Trading could be simple, but believing it was easy turned out to be a gross misunderstanding. Nothing was guaranteed and the work of personal growth required good physical and mental health in order to avoid the many traps that littered the profession like a minefield.

Performance depended on the strength of the three pillars and to get a more vivid vision, I drew and named each of them, giving a particular weight to the psychological aspect. Then, I topped my columns with a lovely cornucopia ... I was pretty proud of my sketches and, to inspire me, I stuck it on the cover of my journal:

The first pillar was called: Preparation and Strategy.

The second: Risk Management.

And the third: Psychological Strength and Discipline.

To be sure, there were traders who did not attach so much importance to these lists and these rules, while enjoying a good performance and a resounding success. To each his own.

But I had to admit frankly that I had a little too artistic a temperament and that I needed such aid. Since childhood, my mind was so creative that if I let myself go, I probably wouldn't be disciplined at all. To top it, my fault of being a little too stubborn was a serious disadvantage... A weakness that I had to lose fast.

I wanted to become a good trader and I already promised myself never to fall asleep on my laurels. When I became successful, I would not start making serious mistakes, once having a routine. My good habits should be well anchored, to never venture on a dangerous path.

Repeatedly, professionals mentioned that the biggest enemy of a trader was hidden in the depths of his soul, but if he remained crushed under the weight of the three pillars, the victory was possible.

Mission "S.M.A.R.T."

To succeed in your mission, you must have single-minded devotion to your goal.

—Abdul Kalam

Steering on my own had not diminished in the least my need to always educate myself and know the tricks of the trade in their infinite details. Actually, my desire to learn was greater.

My many conversations with people working in the business were part of my education and all experienced traders offered the same advice. Clinging to a good capital management, being disciplined and having a prepared plan were the requirements to ensure against a number of problems.

I understood that.

On the trading desk, traders were sitting next to each other and yet, although surrounded by several people, they were really alone with their decisions. I had to be very vigilant about the way I was going to make mine.

When I read a recommendation, I acted only if my research was in agreement with it. If I did not fully understand the benefits or was unable to read into the analyst's words, it was out of the question to follow the advice. It would have been like driving a Lamborghini at 200 km/h, blindfolded. It had nothing exciting for me and I had no intention of running to disaster.

If I was not expected to be an economist, a researcher or a politician, I still had to have sufficient knowledge in all areas to read between the lines of each piece of information.

This was the key to acquiring the little extra that, in addition to the three pillars, would make me a successful trader.

For each transaction, I had to follow a checklist of inevitable steps, including preparation, analysis, strategy, stops, study of the "risk / reward" (decision of acceptable risk and potential profit target written), exit plan and possibly "trailing stops" (stops advancing with price, to help keep more gains).

Each item had to be checked.

Apart from this discipline, staying objective was very important too. Over time, even though I had a pretty good ability to organize, I was flooded with more or less relevant information. I read everything, for fear of missing a detail that would lead to something major. Soon, I had to learn how to filter useful from superfluous to save time.

Thereupon, I wanted to have the vision of my purpose and I decided to project daily, weekly, monthly and yearly goals. From my initial capital and my action plan, I fixed plausible and achievable objectives and I planned to revise these figures eventually, several weeks apart.

Despite my first order for a purchase of ten thousand shares, I preferred small transactions. So I cut my teeth on less risky trades to acquire some trading experience and not let my rookie mistakes leave me traumatized.

I had to establish a process that would produce consistent profits and where, of course, winning trades largely outnumbered losing ones.

So, I decided only to enter into a position if the potential benefit was a point while my stop was placed at a maximum loss of less than half that, to take advantage of every opportunity to win, even if on the whole, I made a profit on only fifty percent of my speculations. The portfolio would still be positive with this method of risk management, which reduced the damage and let the profits accumulate.

The crucial detail was to accept that losses were part of the job. They had to be tolerated but, most importantly, they had to be kept small. Having the discipline to cut the position without hesitation, before things got worse, was vital to limiting any losses. A stop studied in advance was never to be canceled, even for a few minutes, hoping to give "a little more room" to the price. I had heard that a thousand times.

Ahead of time, I wanted to plan my performance objective to reach a profit level that was possible. I needed encouraging figures, which were still feasible. While giving myself smart and thought-through targets, my goal had to be:

S = Specific: With the help of my preparation, good discipline and respect for my rules, I wanted to win "X dollars" in my month, entering small and well studied trades to earn money on a regular basis, and to establish my presence on the desk.

M = Measurable: Register an average of profits amounting to ten thousand dollars a week and $2,000 per day, an amount with which I felt comfortable.

A = Achievable: In light of my recent transactions, my goal was possible, provided that I made no serious mistakes and kept to a balanced risk-return ratio. Without forcing my performance, the potential was there.

R = Relevant: These numbers seemed plausible in their implementation, but not too easy either. This would only be possible if I kept being very vigilant and determined.

T = Tangible: My ambition had to be realized in a set period of time. I promised myself to achieve these goals, for at least four months out of six, which would allow me to finish the year with remarkable profits.

With my mission SMART established, I could evaluate and possibly revise it, to make sure it was in line with my ability, and not an impossible dream that would never materialize.

For this, the profits to risks ratio had to be solid and my work plan viewed, reviewed and verified.

In the near future, if I did not get the desired success, the fault would be caused by poor execution of my mission, in which case the preparation work would have to be improved, until the anticipated gains would substantiate.

My mission was not impossible, and I intended to prove this by making regular transactions, of adequate size for my emotional comfort level, respecting my preparation and staying disciplined about my strategy and my decisions.

This was a recipe that should always be respected.

The best traders agreed unanimously that being stubborn or obstinate and clinging to beliefs or hopes, guaranteed failure and destroyed the chances of success forever.

The market was like the strong wind in the fable of La Fontaine, which had uprooted the oak tree while the reed would just bend over. Bending with the market avoided being destroyed.

To achieve my mission SMART, I had to work on myself, tame my emotional reactions and improve my attitude. Since I was aiming for a career, my life in the business was more important than my ego.

Gradually I was going to acquire the know-how. My self-control and confidence would be established and allow me to impose myself and gain the respect of my colleagues.

For this, I always had to stoop to the market's will.

WORLD TRADE CENTER

*Change is the law of life. And those who look only
to the past or present are certain to miss the future.*

—John F. Kennedy

By early 1993, I was part of the team of rabid wolves of the hedge fund's trading desk and still the only woman.

I totally benefited from my trader status. I was appreciated and respected, not only by Mr. Townsend but also by the members of the trading floor, by the brokers and the business people who knew me. The only difference was that I had never raised my voice or said a vulgar word, just like the big boss.

Hearing them all day annoyed me a bit, but I tried to ignore it while concentrating on my work.

One day in late February, when I picked up the phone to order my lunch, I heard a loud and disturbing noise, like rolling thunder. A short time after the rumble, a line caught my eye on the top of my screen where the news alerts scrolled, informing me of what was happening in the world. It read:

"Explosion at the World Trade Center."

That day, a truck filled with explosives had exploded in the garage. From that moment, I started to look for excuses to leave downtown.

At the beginning of my career as a broker, I had spent three weeks on one of the highest floors of the south tower, in order to train for the broker's business and to learn how to prospect customers. Strangely, at the time, I had felt an unpleasant shiver whenever I entered the elevator. Was it a premonition of what would happen a few years later?

Possibly...

I lived in Manhattan on Central Park South and I had to travel to Wall Street to get to my office. The commute was quite long, a good hour and a half a day, even though I often took the opportunity to come back in the chauffeur-driven Rolls belonging to one of my colleagues, who lived near me.

Actually, I've never enjoyed working far from home, and if I had a choice I would have preferred the center where more and more financial firms had offices. Moreover, almost all the leaders of these lived Uptown (above 57th Street and around Central Park, where my apartment was located). The ideal would have been that the trading desk move, but it would never happen because my boss lived on Long Island and the location of the office was closest for his commute home. Too bad!

On the trading side, I realized that my transactions did not particularly need to be done by a human through the exchange. I did not expect to benefit from improved performance or from getting remarkable help by using floor brokers. With the new technology, it was possible to enter orders electronically, which were executed more quickly.

Of course, getting a "look" from a broker was more descriptive than following the upticks and downticks, but with good preparation, it was not crucial. In fact, I was ready to do without. If only all the boys around me would stop screaming, swearing and insulting each other...

After all this time, I had never said a bad word, only I was wondering if I would not soon begin to talk that way... an idea I refused categorically to accept. These details in themselves were not much, but together they gave me the idea to look elsewhere for a better vibe in general and in particular, an office near me.

I kept the habit of regularly meeting people in the business at their favorite brasserie, and while I was ordering my usual sparkling water, one of them informed me that a former American Stock Exchange specialist had opened a fund he managed with his best traders. The interesting detail was that he was in the process of moving his office to a building not far from my home on Park Avenue.

The location was perfect.

I just had to find out what conditions were offered and what would be my share. There was no question of accepting less than fifty percent of my performance. Although without much hope on the problem of the traders' language, I would have liked it if the people there did not swear as much as those of my office, but it was surely impossible. Market moves had an exciting effect on men, especially on the wild beasts with whom I worked.

The swearing was bothering me a little more each day and I could not understand how they could think while they shouted out their profanities. In addition, I wondered how the brokers could understand the traders properly when they inserted an insult or a vulgarity between every word. I doubted that this habit gave more weight to their words.

At that time, each operator only had one screen showing a list of symbols with their quotes and different links for more indications, news or graphs. But I heard that it would soon be possible to have multiple displays connected to each other, to see all sorts of information and graphs correlated while running many applications. Trading was going to be done on more sophisticated technology, and systems prototypes with extremely fast programs were being developed for the machines to replace humans to a large degree.

Already, computers were being configured for the job and they proved to be excellent traders. Soon, more than 50% of all transactions in the NYSE would be done automatically by robots.

Systems had no afterthought, no hesitation, no emotion and they did not need to be in shape. If the conditions were there, the positions were taken and when the market changed direction, they had no opinion; they were designed to change course or simply cut positions. They were never angry with the market if they took a loss and neither did they feel invincible after generating profits...

REMINISCENCES OF A WALL STREET TRADER

It seemed amazing and I was eager to see what they looked like. I promised myself that once the information was available I would buy my own computer and learn how to configure it, as soon as possible.

Electronic Trading

To improve is to change; to be perfect is to change often.

—*Winston Churchill*

When I called the number of the new trading company I had been told about, I was given an appointment easily. But I preferred to wait until the offices were installed to judge how they would be arranged and most importantly, to make sure it would be possible for me to practice my job effectively. So, I postponed the date until the trading desk was operational.

It was the end of April and the weather was splendid. The sun shone on Manhattan and reflected on the glass facades, dressing buildings with sparkling colors. To attend my meeting with the fund's officials, I decided to walk. Without the need for a coat, I was wearing a dark suit, a white shirt and a man's tie, as always. I felt confident enough and I had no expectations.

Rather, I went there out of curiosity.

In contrast to women who went to work in sneakers and changed upon arriving at the office, I had no problem getting around in high heels. For me, they were more comfortable than flat shoes and, after a most enjoyable stroll, I arrived at the address given to me, relaxed and smiling.

I was greeted by Mr. Rowing, a former specialist and director of the firm, who introduced his partner and walked me through the new floor, where several trading rooms were installed. On the rows of tables, two computer screens were set for each station and the seats were luxurious armchairs of modern appearance. However, only a few were occupied by traders and between each of them, there were several empty places. Unlike on Wall Street, there was no telephone board with direct lines to brokers.

Suddenly, I was shocked to realize the silence reigning on the desk and I looked at my watch. The market was open and yet you could hear a pin drop...

It was incredible!

What a glaring difference to my floor, where at that time there was a tumultuous commotion of a battle, as traders were screaming on the phone.

I was really surprised by the calm surroundings and Mr. Rowing explained that all transactions were done electronically, without the intervention of anyone. The orders were entered on the second machine, directly connected to the exchange. Moreover, without the intervention of any intermediary, the executions were instantaneous and the commissions were much cheaper, a detail appreciable.

Regarding compensation, he offered to pay me seventy percent of the profits I would produce, from a portfolio of five hundred thousand dollars, subject to a thirty thousand dollar guarantee that I had to put up to start. If this amount was to disappear in losses, I would need to add an equal amount in order to continue to trade.

This proposal seemed quite good and, on a handshake, I accepted on the spot.

Thereupon, I went downtown, to my office.

Very unusually, I arrived on Wall Street late in the morning, while the schedule I had adopted over the last two years was to come in at dawn.

Immediately, I asked Mr. Townsend to give me a few minutes when he had a moment. Without waiting, he stood up and invited me to follow him into the small conference room for our conversation to be private.

Since my portfolio had no position at the end of each day and the month was almost over, it would be easy for me to leave. In addition, I kept nothing personal in the office. It was enough to give my resignation and, as usual, the accounting department would transfer my profits payout for the month to my bank account, the first week of May.

Mr. Townsend sat down and I did the same. With appreciation, I thanked him for giving me the chance to learn the trade and assured him that I would never forget that he had belief in me, despite the reluctance of other traders. Also, I told him that my discipline had been especially rigid so as not to disappoint him. I had to leave to be near home and spend more time with my children, instead of making such a long trip every day, but I was sincerely going to miss his influence and presence on the desk and I assured him of my profound gratitude.

He said nothing but stood up, nodding his head to show he understood me very well. I smiled and wanted to kiss him on the cheek, but as I approached closer to him, he put his arms around me with a paternal, short squeeze as if I was his daughter who had just announced she preferred to leave the family home to seek independence.

This burst of tenderness only lasted a second, but his grip had taken me by surprise and my eyes misted.

Stunned and touched, I hastened to bow my head. I did not want him to notice that my admiration had gradually evolved into respectful affection.

I was especially surprised to discover that this iceman could show emotion, despite his distance and his stoic appearance.

So, I left Wall Street and went to continue my trading career in the heart of Manhattan.

COMPUTER

My new trading desk was a haven of peace. Allowing for better concentration, I was sure that my work would benefit and that my performance would be all the better.

From the early days, I liked to walk to my office and I congratulated myself on having made the decision to change funds. This short exercise every morning and afternoon suited me and since it was spring, my walk was most enjoyable.

I discovered that some traders automated their strategies so that many more shares could be analyzed and thus they improved their profits. If I wanted to do the same, I had to get a much more powerful machine than the one I bought for kids.

Thierry, the elder of my sons, had the most interest in the computer and monopolized it. He was passionate about technology and he also spent much of his free time playing with his new camera, practicing taking shots. His talent was evident.

Maxime was excellent at drawing cartoons and had a particular aptitude at karate. His Master had selected him as the best of his school, to perform in a show at Madison Square Garden where children were fighting for the title of black belt, in a televised spin.

I was very proud of my little men!

At the office, I asked the technician who had set up the trading room installation, to deliver urgently a custom built computer. He assembled it with the most efficient parts available at that time and, thanks to its advanced technology and the high speed of its processor, he assured me that it could be programmed with my own trading conditions.

A cabinet was delivered to my home for the "small" sum of eight thousand dollars. It measured three feet high, two feet deep and almost one wide. It was a monster that I was eager to tame or at least to try, but I had first to buy the trading software. I ordered the technical traders' favorite platform, which would allow me to program my formulas. This completed my investment for a total of ten thousand dollars.

Now I still had to get "food" for it, as the in-coming data would provide the necessary figures for my calculations to be done and for that, I paid the monthly charges of the different exchanges in order to analyze every instrument in the comfort of my home, all for about $500 per month. This allowed me to do in-depth analysis on weekends, and improve my work at the office.

The advantage of this method was to test all the formulas in order to obtain a result rated as a percentage of success probability. Thus, all configurations could be reviewed and worked until I arrived at the highest possible proportion of positive results.

With this tool, I could include my techniques and research and create new strategies that would give me signals, according to the conditions stipulated therein. In addition, the platform could execute commands automatically after the programmed technical formulas, which had the advantage of removing all the emotional risks.

The possibilities with all this technology were exciting. However, I had no intention of letting a machine make decisions for me and I had to make sure it was working properly, before trusting it.

To program the assumptions, the use of an "easy language" was necessary and obviously I had to learn it but, contrary to its name, it was so complicated that the platform came with a series of at least ten books, in order to understand how to program the desired conditions. These manuals, some larger than others, explained the operation and were required to "talk" to the application, which is why I launched into this study in the hope of becoming an expert in setting up my new system.

Some trend continuation formulas were fairly easy, but I could also detect them with the naked eye, so the computer did not help me particularly. In addition, I was planning all sorts of strategies and was looking for finding, especially, a reversal signal, a much more complicated task to write effectively.

To verify the quality and expression of my strategies and signals, I could test them historically, up to twenty years back (back-testing), so as to achieve the most efficient system possible.

Thus, when the set conditions were detected, I could see my signals' success potential to buy or sell as a percentage, and work on improving the data until I got a profit score between 75 and 85%.

This occupation fascinated me and I spent every moment of my free time working on this project, knowing that it had the potential to increase my profits.

At first I had no idea that I would spend so much time on this computer, establishing and testing formulas for valid signals. Without suspecting that the process would be so long, week after week, I anticipated being close to the expected results and I thought it would take me just a few more days before reaching my goal.

Three years later, (yes, three years!) I was finally satisfied with the strength and productivity of my method and was proud of my system.

As I had evaluated each indicator and tool, refining them by revised adjustment figures and making them even more compelling, all my trades preparations were much more efficient. Finally, I was able to go Southampton (Long Island) in my time-off and enjoy my Porsche convertible, where there was just enough room for my boys, instead of letting it gather dust in the garage. I was done spending my weekends on my computer, absorbed in developing formulas and tweaking them indefinitely, until they performed perfectly.

I succeeded, at last!

Partnership

*The most important single ingredient in the formula
of success is knowing how to get along with people.*

—*Theodore Roosevelt*

My office was not far from NYU and since my day ended at
about 4 p. m., just after the close of trading, I had time to get to
the University where, after learning in depth the mathematics of
financial analysis, I enrolled once more to continue my education
with the study of Corporate Finance.

I relied on this course to polish my understanding of market
reactions, at a time when mergers and acquisitions had become
numerous, to analyze more intelligently the securities in which I
invested. In fact, when I met business leaders, I did not fail to take
an interest in their projects and I geared the conversation toward the
growth of their sector, to put into practice what I had learned and to
know their point of view and perspective.

Since my departure from the investment bank Paine Webber, I
had always kept in touch with my former clients of the time and
I encouraged each of them to call me if they had any questions on
investment, whether for themselves or for their friends. My advice
was disinterested and my recommendations totally free, since I was
no longer a broker.

The advantage of my position as a trader and the range of my
knowledge were appreciated. Whatever the subject, I had direct
and immediate access to any information necessary to help them.
Increasingly, they asked my opinion, even before accepting a
recommendation from their investment executive.

The children were growing up and had their own interests, which allowed me to exercise more, to have a social life and the opportunity to meet with these investors with whom my friendly relations continued. During these meetings, I listened to them talking about their business and I commented on the general market.

Then, one of them asked me if I was going to open my own money management firm. I replied simply that it was a possibility and if I did, I would let her know. This lady had inherited a huge fortune and I knew her financial contribution would be large.

Why not?

I promised to think about it. However, I earned my living well with trading and I liked the routine of my business. I only had the responsibility of making money, without worrying about public relations and without having to answer to anyone, a freedom that I enjoyed. But frankly, I did not really see any disadvantage to changing my habits and the challenge seemed tempting. However, until I graduated, I could not get involved in the management of an investment group.

Once I completed my studies at NYU and gained my diploma, I decided to start my own partnership, finally interested in this idea of managing money for others. Thus, thanks to the enthusiasm of several potential partners and the encouragement of my colleagues, more than two years after I had started to work at his firm, I asked Mr. Rowing if I could manage my own partnership, on top of my trading.

Without hesitation, he gave me permission.

Once the contracts were ready, I invited all the people I had helped with my advice over the last few years, to invest in my fund, in which I had a large investment myself. While I would continue day trading for Mr. Rowing, this new portfolio was going be operated quite differently and would be managed mostly with swing trades, holding stocks for a few days or a few weeks.

SENIORITY

Fate is nothing but the deeds committed in a prior state of existence.

—*Ralph Waldo Emerson*

Since I had been one of the first traders to enter the premises of Park Avenue, after several years the deans were only Mr. Rowing, his partner and myself. The few men present before my arrival were gone and new ones had appeared, in large numbers, to fill all the seats of the different rooms.

Because of my seniority, each aspirant was sent to me, to get my "short list of trading rules."

I had written it for myself when I started, but I was happy to print it and offer it. I wished the beginners good luck and assured them that I would be ready to help if they needed counsel.

My list took some instructions that traders had long given me, and others that I had learned through experience, with some added information about my approach:

- ✓ Ensure that all information systems are maintained and upgraded. Restart the computer before the first trade.

- ✓ Never listen to tips! The risks are unknown and can't be managed intelligently.

- ✓ Do your research the night before or early in the morning, before the opening of the market, and be prepared.

- ✓ Check the economic calendar to avoid being trapped by a market reaction causing a sudden adverse move.

✓ Start each day with a positive mindset, "Your attitude determines your altitude."

✓ Develop a method to keep up morale (Pep Talk and Relaxation).

✓ Think like a warrior ... No prayer, no hope, only the strategy matters!

✓ Do not trade when tired or upset. The acronym H.A.L.T. comes from Hungry, Angry, Lonely or Tired. These are conditions that negatively affect trading.

✓ Do not act on recommendations or professional advice, unless you have verified the information through personal experience, technical analysis and other sources.

✓ Do not risk more than 1 or 2% of capital on each trade.

✓ Associate technical analysis with fundamental reasons.

✓ In a bull market, one can only be bullish (Buy).

✓ An uptrend stock may only be sold short on a bounce back after a gap down (with exceptions).

✓ If news is published in a magazine about an investment, do not touch it. It is too late; the facts are known and the movement is already done.

✓ A market that does not go up on good news is surely tired and probably about to fall in value.

✓ In general, avoid trading against the trend, but in exceptional cases that anticipate a reversal, caution must be particularly high and the stop tight.

✓ Being able to adapt is vital. Consider designing and implementing a new trading plan if the current market conditions become uncomfortable.

✓ Compare the behavior of other companies' shares in the same sector. The relative strength is very important. Always trade the leader of a group.

✓ Do not try to do something big. It is best to win gradually and safely. Taking less risk can help make more. Earning 1% profit per week brings up the capital gain by more than 60% per year!

✓ Take small positions to be able to make clear and profitable decisions (no stress helps keeping cool).

✓ If a stock opens upwards with a gap that is not filled half an hour after opening, the force is real, and buying is advisable.

✓ Try to go in the direction of the opening, with a stop placed just below the previous day's close.

✓ Gap up, put a buy order at half the gap and exit if the price turns negative.

✓ It is normal for a strong market to correct its initial move with a retracement of half its advance or more... This is an opportunity to enter.

✓ Do not change the selection filters, unless they have been tested and the new formula has a return above 75% average gain, compared to the risk. Ideally it's 85%.

✓ Follow the checklist of the trading method or strategy for each transaction before entry. If one of the conditions is missing, cancel the idea to trade.

✓ Stops should be placed over the resistance for sell orders and below the support for purchase orders.

✓ Do not answer the phone during the execution of a trade. Stay focused on it.

✓ Check that the correct confirmation is received for each order.

✓ If the market opened sharply down, close your short position at the open and later, decide to sell it again at a higher price after a retracement or bounce back (for positions kept overnight).

✓ If a gap in price against the position is not closed by lunchtime, get out (short term trading). It shows a real force in that direction. First, exiting frees the mind from looking at a loss and secondly, it allows you to reassess the situation with clear thoughts. But if a gap is closed within the first two hours, hold on to the position until the stop is hit.

✓ Market down, note the positive stocks, which will perform better when the market turns up. The strength of a security relative to the market or its industry is very indicative.

✓ No "Yes, but..." or "If only..." or even "Maybe..." No opinion... No excuses... Discipline!

✓ Have no emotion! Fear, panic, greed or euphoria will lead to errors.

✓ Taking quick profits is not a mistake; it is what day trading is all about.

✓ Never add to a losing position.

✓ Taking a small loss frees the mind and allows you to focus on other positions of merit, not to mention that it saves you from taking a big loss.

✓ Never be without a stop, correctly positioned.

✓ Do not let a profit turn into a loss. Keep your stop in place and try to get to breakeven as soon as possible, getting out of half and leaving the other half to profit without any risk.

✓ Avoid taking small profits and big losses: accept quickly being wrong.

✓ Let profits run and move the stop if a new strategic level protects it.

✓ A stock split announcement is positive; a reverse stock split is negative (day trading).

✓ The most dangerous words in trading are "It's gone too far!" In reality, it can go much further.

✓ In case of a modification of the usual procedures, write it in your journal and highlight the reasons for the change. The rules of the strategy are to be followed and should not be ignored.

✓ Stop trading for some time if: - the operating account has fallen below 35% compared to the beginning of the year - five consecutive trades were losing - you feel negative, uncertain or bored - you are tired, ill, upset, pressed for time or otherwise distracted - or when trying to compensate for previous losses.

✓ Do not go back and enter the same trade out of spite once stopped out. Chances are the price will go further and another loss will occur. Plan your trade.

✓ When in doubt ... Get out!

✓ If a news announcement is expected, get out of half the position even if there is a high chance of positive results, (good or bad, there will be less exposure or risk).

✓ Do not keep a position before the announcement of significant figures.

✓ Check if the reasons for your entry are still valid and if your trade still performs as expected, at least once every hour (day-trading).

✓ At the end of the week, examine and analyze each closed transaction and review all log entries.

✓ Follow the rules until you are qualified enough to know when to break them.

LBO Introduction

The key to growth is the introduction of higher dimensions of consciousness into our awareness.

—Lao Tzu

A few years earlier, back when I was a broker at Hamilton Grant, I had asked my manager if it was possible for me to work in corporate mergers and acquisitions, since there was an M & A department in the firm.

I must say that before discovering the potential of the biotechnology company, I had a hard time selling the firm's products and I was hoping to get another position in the company. He answered it was impossible and inferred I should focus on opening new accounts by selling the famous "penny-stocks."

Shortly after, during my interview with the Playboy reporter, most of the questions had been about my job, but one of them was different:

"What are your dreams?"

I had replied without hesitation and without even thinking: "Work in mergers and acquisitions, find Prince Charming and merge with him…"

Regarding the Prince… We met a lot later and I've never been so happy as since my marriage to David, a caring man, extremely knowledgeable, whom I admire. But that's another story, which we'll come to later.

As for my interest back then in corporate mergers, it was a hope that my job as a trader and portfolio manager made me forget. I had long since accepted that a job in M & A was an impossible dream.

However, the words written above the blackboard of my childhood classroom came back to me from time to time, like an echo:

"When we want, we can!"

During my studies in Corporate Finance and in mathematics for financial analysis, I was fascinated by the LBO (Leveraged Buy Out - Acquisition with leverage). Moreover, large fortunes were born through the use of this method and I met several people who had benefited greatly from it.

By definition, this principle was to invest a fraction of the acquisition of a company, rarely more than 10% of its value, and to finance the vast majority by using a bank or bond issuance, which resulted in increasing the return on equity. The debt from the acquisition, whether banking or not, was repaid by a greater drain on the acquired company's revenues.

In the partnership where I was now managing investments, a large inflow of funds came from a certain Mr. Jackson.

He was a serious and authoritative man, extremely intelligent, and also full of common sense. He had founded and was the owner of a company which manufactured fiberglass, using machines to weave it, to make the material that would be the basis for the making of electronic boards, computer circuit boards, bulletproof vests for police, soldiers' helmets, the insides of aircraft and, I believe, the shell bodies of some cars.

The company was considered as part of the textile industry and thus belonged to the same sector as those producing clothes or carpets. Therefore, it was estimated at the performance coefficient of that industry and was far from the value projection of technology companies, which were soaring in the market.

All IPOs with any connection, near or far, to computers or the Internet, were blazing incredibly at this time. Their market price opened higher every day, sometimes doubling in value on the first day of issuance.

In the spring of 1995, during a lunch with Mr. Jackson, I presented him the idea of a buyout of his company, but he indicated that the industry was not in demand and no one was interested, although the expansion of his business was excellent.

Despite his somewhat negative reaction, I insisted that a buyout could be highly profitable if his enterprise were presented, not as part of the textile industry, but as a support industry for the manufacture of computers and mobile phones.

I also thought that the part fiberglass played in providing safety equipment for the military, with the war going on in Bosnia, could attract interest.

Unfortunately, I did not manage to convince him in the least, notwithstanding my arguments and my enthusiasm... His response was limited to agreeing that I could make approaches for a buyout. He had no expectation of any interest or success.

I had the presence of mind at this point to ask if I would be entitled to a commission, if my idea succeeded and a profitable transaction was concluded.

He did not hesitate to shake hands with me, answering:

"Absolutely!"

I was delighted and, as always, my inner voice reminded me that determination would define my destiny. For me, the risk was nil and the profit potential significant.

With one more project aside from my trading and the new evening classes in which I had just enrolled to study economics at the New School in New York, I had no time to get bored.

Getting interviews to present my project was quite difficult because I was not the employee of an investment bank and I had no connection with a corporate finance department. Most investment funds refused to meet with me, and with the few appointments I was able to get, I recorded multiple defeats. But I was resolute and tenacious. My attempts to introduce the project differently also proved unsuccessful and these alternatives had led to nothing. But, not for a moment, did I have any idea of giving up.

And, as always, it was enough to knock on the right door. A year later, an LBO was completed.

The "deal" was signed for an acquisition amounting to over $192 million.

I had no contract guaranteeing my commission, and yet I received the biggest check of my life, with a letter of congratulations for bringing the company to the leaders of venture capital funds.

Moreover, the idea was so good that, only thirty-six months later, in 1998, the company was sold for $485 million, much to the delight of Mr. Jackson's family and all the company's directors, who had entered loans themselves to participate in the investment and were, therefore, amply rewarded.

My dream to work on corporate mergers had been realized without ever working for a specialized firm.

Obviously, I had great luck and, once again, the inspiration of the words above the blackboard in my classroom had crowned my hopes with success.

To celebrate this victory, I gathered all my family in Paris and invited them to a cabaret. To everyone, I gave a large check as a gift and the evening was excellent. I was really happy to share my good fortune with them.

All these years, I had always been very discreet about the worries of my early life in New York and my difficulty in filling my children's needs. No one knew anything about my problems, and I was too proud ever to cry about my circumstances to my parents, or to confide in my brothers or sister. Moreover, they considered me rather distant, far beyond the Atlantic Ocean separating us.

Since I had married very young and had left France more than ten years earlier, I was hoping that this visit would bring me closer to them and my gifts would be a way to express how I loved them dearly.

I had to return to the United States and I did not have time to go shopping for all of them, so I imagined they would prefer to have the pleasure of choosing what they wanted to buy. I was happy about that and was just hoping that my intention would be understood as a token of affection and not an opportunity to brag about my success.

Back in New York, I bought for cash a beautiful apartment on the twenty-second floor of the Hampshire House, a building with a green and pitched roof, so pretty it was on all the Central Park postcards. However, the layout of parts of my new home was not perfectly according to my taste and I decided to have some wall partitions moved. Thus, the kitchen was enlarged so that it looked like that of a house, ultra modern and white with blue-gray granite that looked like silver nuggets. Then I designed my dream bathroom to double the space, adding a Jacuzzi, like a pink marble seashell.

For the renovation to be complete, I also changed all the windows, which forced me to go and live in the Club-Hotel at the corner of Fifth Avenue and 60th for two months, while the kids were in camp. My only disappointment in our lovely apartment was not being able to use the large fireplace in the living room, which could only be used as decoration, due to the real estate laws in the area.

The work was very important, but the result was so spectacular, that I congratulated myself for being patient ...

It was a quality I had learned by trading.

Hedge Fund Creation

The creation of a thousand forests is in one acorn.

—Ralph Waldo Emerson

When I finally finished my economics class at the New School, I felt ready to get serious and I successfully closed down the investment partnership that I managed to replace it with a hedge fund. I had waited to have a little more time to devote myself one hundred percent to climb this new step in my career.

Although it was a challenge, I felt ready and I trusted I be up to this advance.

To install the fund, I was considering the acquisition of a new office and hiring staff, but I had the idea of first visiting my clearing house to ask what the conditions would be to establish my office there and I learned that they would welcome me free. Of course, they knew how much commission I paid through their order system and that I was a very good customer.

I thanked them but, before making a decision, I decided to talk to the leaders of my firm. As I had led the management of my partnership fund for several years, I was hoping they would agree to let me continue to negotiate on their premises. The problem was that I had no intention of working on their behalf in day trading and I suspected they would surely see a disadvantage.

My argument was that all the commissions I generated electronically for my transactions were shared between the clearing house and Mr. Rowing's firm.

My departure would have terminated these inflows of money and I was hoping to convince them to accept, and to keep on receiving their share of the commissions I paid using their machines orders, a figure representing a very high amount that they would not get if I went elsewhere.

I had good arguments and they accepted, although they were a bit disappointed.

The company was going to move to much larger offices. The number of traders was quickly approaching hundreds and many branches had been opened recently, scattered in several cities of the United States.

The bastion of the company being New York, the new headquarters were chosen at a fancy address and belonged to the heart of the giant canyon of glass and concrete that was Avenue of the Americas. The entrance was at the corner of Fiftieth Street and the trading rooms occupied several stories above Rockefeller Center. I liked the location, only a ten minute walk away from my apartment.

Mr. Rowing occupied the large corner office on the left wing and invited me to take a similar space on the right wing, as his partner had preferred to stay among all the other traders whom he supervised, in rooms lined with long rows of computer stations.

The two large windows in my office opened onto a magnificent view of the Plaza, which during winter became an ice rink and turned into a beautiful flower garden at summer time. However, with my five screens, it was rare for me to look outside and besides, the blinds were always half lowered so that the sunlight would not glare on my monitors and make them much less readable.

A television connected to financial news was suspended near the ceiling, although I just listened to it, my eyes busy with quotes flashing, lines of written information scrolling and graphs moving rapidly.

Once installed, I could start the process and create my fund with authorization to perform alternative management and ask lawyers to establish the charter and the contracts. I put the minimum amount to invest at seven hundred and fifty thousand dollars, which seemed a very reasonable amount to me and I invited in priority all the partners in my old partnership.

My initial contribution was high. It was the same principle as before, the only difference being that this time I was authorized to negotiate futures and options. However, all my transactions would remain, for a time, with shares traded on the New York Stock Exchange.

Thus the Viking Hedge Fund was born.

With the agreement of the firm's leaders, I could use the accounting reports received from the back office and therefore hardly had any fixed costs. That is why I decided not to charge any annual management fees and my compensation remained limited to the usual twenty percent payout from my profits.

As always, I kept an eye on the news showing on one of my screens and I traded what I had prepared in my trading plan, keeping on trading only stocks throughout the first year.

I entered all my orders electronically and also, I had the opportunity to use a platform "Instinet" allowing me to consult large size offers from banks and funds, to trade directly with them.

I liked my new office.

There were no direct lines and my orders had not been through floor brokers of the stock exchange for a long time, but some of them had become my friends and I had the pleasure of meeting them often. Over the months, they gave me tips more than once but, to the astonishment of the other traders who knew nothing of the lesson of my first trade, I never followed any.

I was used to the signals of my system, which indicated the possibility of buying and selling and which were quite valuable to help me get a decent performance. These alerts could also flash danger, to avoid getting into trades with less potential.

To practice my work efficiently, it was necessary to have a number of screens which allowed me to see the behavior of different instruments at the same time, since there was often a correlation between them. Also, the observation of the same stock viewed on several time frames allowed me to check my assumptions, with an overview of its activity.

And, thanks to my studies in economics and financial analysis, I was able to add research to my decision process and, eventually, to seek investments in certain sectors before confirming the found possibilities with technical analysis, which added timing to choose the right moment. As such, I could accumulate a large number of success probabilities to my choice of transaction.

At that time, an excellent platform was beginning to be particularly popular. It was created by Michael Bloomberg[3] and cost about fifteen hundred dollars a month but had the especially valuable advantage of having been designed by a trader, for traders. It offered all the tools that an operator would wish for.

Bloomberg had been one of the great traders of the firm Salomon Brothers and, after his dismissal, he used his ten million dollars severance pay to create the most powerful platform, with a great news service, extensive fundamental analysis and remarkable information.

Only for my technical trading, I had to keep my system because my graphs were much more efficient, thanks to the formulas I had invented, but they could not be used on this display. Anyway, I was thinking of adding an extra screen for a Bloomberg, the machine having taken the name of its creator.

At the end of my first year of business, I was doing well. I did not get amazing results, but I held the road, being extremely cautious and taking the least risks possible, despite a highly bullish environment.

My reserve was caused by the euphoria surrounding the technology shares and, particularly, those of Internet companies, which were flying a little too high for my liking. Over the weeks, I began to sense the market overheating perilously and the buyers' enthusiasm made me feel increasingly uncomfortable.

My instinct felt danger.

---

3 Michael Bloomberg amassed a large fortune, and later was elected mayor of New York on several occasions.

BUYING GOLD

Successful investing is anticipating the anticipations of others.

—*John Maynard Keynes*

At the beginning of the summer 1999, everyone was talking about Y2K.

The New Year was a few months away and rumors went around that at midnight, on December 31st, computers might not work properly, since they were not built with the ability to adapt to the millennium, bringing the date to 2000 and changing its first digit. The world having become dependent on machines, major problems were anticipated.

Although the magnitude of the expected complications seemed exaggerated, this kind of reasoning provoked reactions. There were mixed views and opinions argued. Yet, one indicator of the market health seemed to have difficulty climbing, while the SP500 advanced regularly. The advance/decline line of the securities comprising this benchmark did not confirm its rise and its "breath" was poor. It was not dramatic, but was to be considered as a red flag.

In general, my information was obtained on one of my five screens, reserved in part to the news scrolling down all day, although I happened to look up to watch TV for an instant, if a friend of mine was interviewed.

For many years, I got used to just read the beginning of the each line of news and to understand its meaning almost half-word while, of course, my attention was focused on the graphs, which I followed very closely, and on the quotes, which gave me the market pulse.

One July day, early in the afternoon, a sentence was intriguing enough for me to move my mouse and click on it, in order to open its linked window and read its contents.

"Possible bankruptcies among gold producers…"

I did not trade gold and I still had not touched the futures market, but their prices appeared on my platform.

In any case, the reason for these failures interested me. After an historic high (to date) in January 1980, the yellow metal had entered a dramatically bear market, losing 70% of its value over the last nineteen years and Gold was now quoted at $257 per ounce.

What particularly piqued my curiosity was why the assumption of these failures was anticipated. While the cost to extract the precious metal from the soil was estimated to average $250 an ounce, if it traded at only a few dollars more, it would not be profitable any longer, for most producers, to mine it. Therefore, there would be less gold taken out of the ground…

Hence, the potential for a price increase.

Deep inside, I knew it was the kind of detail that could yield a lot of money. A common, seemingly unimportant piece of information, which had the potential to change the direction of a terrifying bear market.

Furthermore, with doubt and questions raised about Y2K, this idea seemed particularly interesting.

Despite this, I had to admit to not having any experience on the trading of precious metals or commodities in general, far from it. Among my many other trading licenses, the "Series 3" for commodities did not reassure me enough to undertake a straight futures purchase.

After making sure all my positions were protected by stops placed at improved strategic levels, my mind was free to study the risks and profits potential of a gold position. It was out of the question to buy gold futures directly as I considered the risks of an entry on this basis way too high to trade them, while their volume was sporadic. Less conceivable and even more dangerous was to acquire shares of companies mining gold, since some of them could go bankrupt.

I spent that afternoon considering the best way to participate in a possible bullish reversal. The graph appeared to head into the abyss and it seemed impossible to predict when and where the price would stop its descent.

In fact, the cause for the implacable bear market was fairly commonplace.

Gold had been tumbling relentlessly for several years, but it was the doing of central banks who, with their mountains of gold in deposit, did not want to keep any asset not bearing interest. Consequently, they were eager to get rid of it, like a dead weight. So gold, so to speak, had no interest for these banks, which sold the metal constantly to replace their reserves with profitable instruments.

Until that day, my formulas had only been applied to stocks. Therefore, without further ado, I began to add commodities to my trading system, to analyze the price of the precious metal.

One of my new signals had taken an extremely long time before being considered effective, but eventually had shown a success rate of over 85%, although it rarely appeared. Unlike those I used regularly, it was designed specifically to indicate the possibility of a trend reversal. In the formula, there were so many conditions that I thought it would never indicate anything.

And yet... Hello!

The weekly chart of gold showed a buy, which had formed on the previous week. Of course the bar or candle had to be closed for the signal to be visible, so it was mainly after Friday's closing, or on weekends, that I was scanning my charts.

Logically, on a longer-time interval, the warnings had more weight. But I had not seen that one, because until now, I only followed stocks. Still, I wondered if I would have acted on that alert without having read the news, which had given me a hint. So, it was time to act although, certainly, I was going to sail in rather hostile waters.

To negotiate commodities, there was no electronic trading. I had to create an additional account for the execution and delivery of the contracts, in exchange for cash settlement. Although my portfolio was authorized to trade futures, it had only contained shares and a special account had to be created and added, to enter this unusual position. Immediately, I called my clearing house's execution services and opened a futures account, which would show the order I was going to give directly to the Comex broker standing near the gold pit, where it was exchanged.

Trades would be delivered against payment, like in the days when I worked with Mr. Townsend. Although this detail delayed establishing my position by twenty-four hours, everything went smoothly. I intended to buy hundreds of options contracts on futures and I needed long-term Calls, since it was impossible to determine how much time would pass, before a significant slowdown in production would result in a rise in price.

This position seemed pretty risky, but intuitively, I thought it was OK. A few times before in my life, I had felt an odd sensation in my stomach that told me that I absolutely had to act, and that day, I sensed that. Without any assurance that my reasons were infallible, I really believed in them.

But I wanted to know exactly how much I could lose and I did not intend to waste a penny more, which is why I bought Calls options to cover the entire value of this investment. Indeed, I risked losing the full amount if, by the expiration date of my options, gold was not over $280. My total bet was nearly a quarter of a million dollars and I adopted an "all or nothing" approach, to win big or lose it all on this idea.

This position represented a ton of gold.

And then, of course, as was way too common with options, the value of my Calls began to decrease as soon as they were in my portfolio. In fact, from the first day, their value began to lose quite quickly. Determined, despite the obvious deterioration, I intended to hold on to it, even if the Calls went to zero. I was resolute that I would wait until the contracts expired, and that was many months away.

By August, my investment was estimated as losing a hundred thousand and by September, my set back was over one hundred and fifty thousand dollars.

I needed nerves of steel to contemplate the money evaporate that fast, but truth be told, I had them.

At the office, some traders knew I had bet on this option and sometimes they looked at me puzzled, apparently wondering if I had not lost my mind. However, no one dared to comment. As for me, I deliberately did not want to think about the danger of my speculation and I decided to trust my logical mind, accepting that the cost of my assumption amounted to a quarter million dollars.

One Monday morning in early fall, I had a shock when I arrived at the office. I could not believe my eyes!

Gold had risen twenty percent with a huge gap from its previous closing price. It happened after the announcement of the Washington Agreement, signed between several central banks, to refrain from selling more than 400 tons of gold per year, and to stick to this for the next five years.

In the futures market, an increase of 2% allowed an initial investment to double. With a price increase of 20%, the value of my Calls on gold futures was multiplied exponentially!

My profits were incredible.

Pensive and silent, I was trying to decide if I should get out of this position immediately or wait a few days to see what would happen. In any case, I had to work my position with the help from my broker on the COMEX, although the surprise showed such a huge bid that I could have sold my entire quantity in one order. I had to be fast enough to take advantage of this reaction, which gave me an advantage over those who had to cover their short position urgently, as they had lost a lot of money and the "Margin Clerks" were going to force their hand.

They were buyers and luckily, I had a good amount to offer. Since my first day in the business, I knew that a gap often got filled... So, I had to sell soon enough.

I always kept the double doors to my office wide open, my back to the entrance; it allowed new traders to come closer to ask my advice without the need to knock on my door. If I felt a presence when I was too busy, I simply raised my hand, which meant to come back later.

While I pondered, lost in my thoughts, a trader from one of the other office floors, a tall and jovial man and a good friend of Mr. Rowing's partner, came to visit me.

I turned from my screens to greet him with a smile when, suddenly, he knelt before me and said fervently…

"Will you marry me?"

Taken aback, I did not move for a second, before bursting out laughing. I was not the only one who had read the announcement on gold!

My eyes tearing with amusement as I tried to stop, I thanked him profusely. I knew he was married with five children, but I appreciated the joke and I was not only entertained, but touched.

His gesture was delightfully funny and I perceived it as a nice compliment, while brightening me with his unexpected humor. When he left, it took me a while to stop laughing.

It was this event (the gold, not the proposal!) that propelled my career to a higher level and prompted me to trade futures with more regularity.

During the presentation of the quarterly results of my funds, my investors were thrilled and many of them added significant amounts to expand their participation. My reputation was established and then, thanks to my outstanding overall performance, new people would contact me, without my needing to solicit, to entrust me with a portion of their financial assets.

My funds widened significantly and, more than ever, I had to take into account the macroeconomic situation and diversify my portfolio.

Boston Globe

When the legend becomes fact, print the legend.

—The Man Who Shot Liberty Valence

At that time, everyone was talking about the "dot.com" and the fabulous rise of technology stocks, marveling at their potential. When some criticized the unfairly high price of companies earning no profits, the phrase in vogue was:

"This time is different ..."

As the year 2000 was getting closer, the Internet bubble swelled visibly and a greater number of folks were attracted by the huge profits they heard others brag about, ignoring the mounting risks that the Nasdaq would collapse. People were afraid to miss the boat and wanted to jump on board, to win at this game. Even the shoeshine boys in the underpass of Rockefeller Center spoke of latest tips to buy "dot.com" stocks which would surely double in value, in no time.

At the office, new traders came in larger numbers to try day-trading with the intention to profit from the market's constant rise. But they often lost their thirty thousand dollars and, if they could not add the cash amount to cover their guarantee, they had to leave and make room for new aspirants. They learned the hard way that short-term trading was very difficult.

One morning in November, Mr. Rowing asked me if I would be willing to answer questions from a reporter who was writing an article on women day-traders. Even though I was now independent, he thought that by agreeing to meet someone from the press on the subject, it would be good publicity for his firm.

I replied cheerfully:

"With pleasure ..."

The appointed day, a young woman from the Boston Globe appeared at the reception, and immediately I invited her into the conference room. After I had been interviewed for a few minutes, she asked me if she could stay with me until the close of the market, to see how I was trading. I replied with a smile:

"Of course!"

She followed me to my desk and, once she was sitting comfortably next to me, I explained what I was looking for in the market and showed her my order machine on which I created a separate account from the rest of my portfolio, so she could judge my gains and my losses live, as they occurred.

Thereupon I went to work.

During the afternoon, my trading was fast and on different stocks, with positions held only a few minutes. And then, all my transactions were closed just before the New York Stock Exchange closing bell, a signal heard on the financial news TV program.

Without a word, the reporter took notes following my activities for her report and she verified that the result was indeed a profit of nearly nine thousand dollars, net of all commissions.

Visibly impressed, she congratulated me and, several days later, a few copies of the Boston Globe were delivered to my office. An article, published on Saturday November 13th, 1999 entitled "Women Day-Trading dawns on Wall Street" was on the front page, with my picture taken while I was trading actively.

The photograph clearly showed the "Discipline" sign hanging on one of my five screens and when I noticed this detail was visible, I imagined with amusement Mr. Townsend's reaction, the one who taught me how to trade and that too, of the hungry wolves around him. Years had gone by and since that time, I had not had any contact with my mentor, but I always kept my apprenticeship in memory and my gratitude was profound.

If I had become a great trader, it was due to him and all my life, I'd be thankful.

ARROGANCE AND STUBBORNNESS

Nothing is more obstinate than a fashionable consensus.

—Margaret Thatcher

The new millennium was fast approaching and I was increasingly wary of the market's behavior. The Nasdaq seemed especially dangerous and bloated by blind enthusiasm, which had propelled upwards some worthless technology companies in that index, as if they were the new Microsoft or the new Intel. I was convinced that this overvaluation would end in tragedy, but I seemed to be the only one to worry about it.

Purely speculatively, the price of the many "dot.com" climbed more each day and hundreds of stocks went rising to the sky, while there were no foundations to their survival.

Some Internet companies reporting no profit were priced according to the number of people who visited their website, without ever buying anything.

Any new idea of business creation through the Web was expected to develop into a profitable enterprise, and even if the chances of success were imaginary and extrapolated into the future, this possibility multiplied the price of their IPO and brought considerable demand. People were investing in mirages, looking for the "startup" who would win, as if it were a raffle in which they would get the winning number.

Apparently, nobody could fathom that this folly would not last and perceive the possibility that the music would eventually stop playing.

Aside from my short-term trading, I entered into positions for longer periods, which occupied a large part of my portfolio and for which my decisions were rather taken initially from fundamental analysis. Only, I was far less efficient with this. In fact, my results were poor, compared to those generated through technical analysis where my transactions were of short duration, while allowing me to reuse the funds to earn much more profits with the same capital. The value of my portfolio being considerably higher, I had to invest in highly liquid positions when I traded short term.

Since my training, I had often heard that a trader must remain humble. If he became arrogant, the market always found a way to get him off his pedestal, giving him a lesson he would not soon forget... But, as my career and reputation soared, I got the feeling I could never do wrong.

Towards the end of 1999, the meteoric rise of the Nasdaq market made me nauseous and I speculated that if it were to fall, it would certainly take the other indices with it. Therefore, I was on the lookout for any sign announcing a top, although almost all my trades were with securities traded on the New York Stock Exchange, where the values were not as overheated... Except one, which annoyed me particularly.

When that company released its quarterly report, I was furious. I did not believe a word of it and I considered its figures as lies meant as a personal insult.

Enron was the most popular NYSE stock and its market trend was most positively bullish, but I had an almost physical aversion to it.

While its graph inferred to buy it, I wanted to sell. But, of course, every time I entered into a bearish bet, I suffered a loss, which I considered an affront. The humiliation poisoned my thinking and festered disgust; I was beside myself.

On several occasions, the price appeared to be toppy, but my vision was obstructed by my desire and I could not get the fair interpretation of its real behavior. Of course, when I entered a short position, the price declined a bit to go my way as if teasing me, just before advancing more fiercely to touch my stop and make me lose money, again.

I was running out of patience; I felt so strongly that this stock was a fake, I wanted to capitalize on the very large drop in value that was inevitable (only in my mind). I was forgetting that the greatest danger was to trade while disturbed.

This was going against my strategies, against what I learned from the beginning, against common sense, discipline and all reason.

Far from ignoring how hurtful negative emotions were to trading, I was accumulating them, including anger and a bruised ego. I had learned to tame my stubbornness; however the pressure was too strong and I was forgetting all my good resolutions. Also, I was convinced that the new year 2000 would cause some disruption, notwithstanding that the market had become ridiculously expensive. I felt justified; the indices had to go down and they could not stay inflated indefinitely.

In addition, Enron was not worth much, I was certain.

I had always been a tad reckless, but reflective nonetheless. Then again, my trade in gold might have spoiled me. With my great results, I felt it had become easy for me to earn money and, since I was not in the habit of being wrong, I became very bold.

Despite not finding any reason dictated by technical analysis to sell Enron short, my thirst for vengeance became a need.

Regardless of whether I was ahead of the graph, I did not doubt for a moment that the sell signal would come sooner or later... I knew I was betting against the trend; doing that was very dangerous. Indeed, the higher the price went up, the more I could lose, but I was determined to take a position now, for the long term.

With the purchase of securities, the risk was that the value goes to zero, since the total amount of the acquisition was the maximum to be lost. In contrast, when short selling, the price could double, triple or multiply by a thousand; and therefore, the risks are unlimited.

In November, Enron began to lose a little value and, encouraged, I sold the stock at $40, for a total sum of one million dollars. A twenty-five thousand shares order was not an unusual amount for my fund, although, this was at the high end of the spectrum, the size of my capital requiring positions averaging ten thousand shares. So far, my yearly results were excellent and I could afford to take on more risks, or so I thought.

I had the arrogance not to see for an instant what a blatant error this was and I neglected the notion that a major trading pitfall was to think that the price had gone too far. In fact, I was ignoring one of my own warnings to beginners. A price could reach a level unthinkable before returning to "equilibrium."

I often quoted John Maynard Keynes, who had said:

"Markets may remain illogical far longer than you and I may remain solvent."

Decidedly stubborn, I established my position with the intention of keeping it.

In mid-December, my loss on Enron was small and I enjoyed excellent yearly results, with my profits on gold and my superior performance throughout the previous quarters. Serene, I invited my parents to meet me in Florida to spend three weeks with the children in a large house with a swimming pool, located in one of the finest country clubs of the area.

I went to pick them up at Miami airport in a chauffeured limousine and I welcomed them with many gifts. Golf, tennis, shopping, every day was a pleasure and for Christmas, I organized a four-day cruise on a large ship. Also, back on the mainland, we celebrated New year's Eve 2000 in a gastronomic restaurant with a ballroom, to begin the millennium in style.

I had planned every detail for the enjoyment of my family reunion and this holiday in the sun was simply unforgettable.

Back in New York, Enron was still recommended by all the analysts, more than ever. The price had gone up, but I had lost all discipline and refused to exit my position. Worse, I was unable to focus on anything else, doing nothing but watching the quote. I had not placed a stop and all that I had learned was erased from my memory. My faculty to discern hard facts was blinded by my stubbornness and my hatred for the stock.

Two or three weeks later, I was bedridden with terrible flu, keeping me away from my screen for a few days, but this problem was insignificant compared to what was happening in my short position. Enron had nearly doubled in value since my entry, and it could still get worse.

I lost a fortune.

Thus, despite my original intention to keep the position a very long time, I was forced to take losses absolutely huge. It was not only dramatic for my morale, but also my capital. As for the value of the company, the price continued to rise, and every day, the enthusiasm of buyers was increased.

It was only a few months later, at the end of that summer 2000, that the fraud, which had seemed obvious to me, was discovered and that doubts began to enter investors' minds. The price of Enron, whose top had been only ten points above the level at which I had quit holding on to it, finally began to crumble.

Thus, as a poorly closed red balloon, its air escaped and its value began to deflate relentlessly to reach zero a year later.

The Darling of Wall Street was no longer.

However, I was not comforted in the least. I had been right, but my timing had been completely wrong. My gravest mistake was to have let myself be carried away by exasperation, by rage and by ego. All I had rehearsed for years never to do, had been consigned to oblivion and I had acted like a beginner.

Obviously, I deserved to pay the price to learn the biggest lesson of my trader life.

While a good discipline and careful preparation before each trade had grown my capital and rewarded me with the esteem of all, a moment of stupidity, a lack of reflection, a feeling of arrogance and a sense of invincibility, resulted in the loss of weeks of work and an amount of money that would take time before it could be recovered.

But worst of all, when my research and technical analysis finally gave me the green light to sell short, when the time was right, I did not want to touch it, disgusted by Enron once and for all. I even removed its symbol from my screens, so as not even to see it.

Thus, not only had I lost a million dollars, but nor did I win when the time was appropriate and my system flashed the descent. I could have made up all my losses and some, only I was scalded and unable to trade this value. Consequently, I did not take part in Enron's dramatic decline.

To succeed, we have to follow what the market dictates and simply obey its law; otherwise, failure is assured. Trading was winning when we went in the direction of the opinion of the mass, and that is why the favorite phrase among traders was indeed:

"The trend is your friend."

I was deeply ashamed at having fallen into destructive emotions.

This should never, not ever, have happened to me!

The morality of this terrible experience was not to insist on going in one direction if the price proved going the other way and to have stops to exit a bad trade. Since only the price was right, it was going to dictate the trader's behavior and indicate the path to take. Woe to the one who dared to go against it!

The flow of money was the greatest ally...

Nasdaq-QQQ

There is no better than adversity. Every defeat,
every heartbreak, every loss, contains its own seed,
its own lesson on how to improve your performance the next time.

—Malcolm X

At the beginning of the new millennium, my performance was pitiful and my first quarter had started really badly.

Enron, whose quote had captured my attention, had cost too much time. I now had to regain my discipline, roll up my sleeves and go to work, taking my courage in both my hands. I had shown enough nonsense to last a lifetime and I had to get back to trade seriously.

Thus, once rid of this ridiculous position, I resumed my good habits and proceeded again as I knew how. Obviously, I did not want to try to make up for my losses too quickly, knowing that this was the best way never to get there. Slowly but surely was the only way to proceed.

Individually, Nasdaq shares did not interest me in the least. Even though many of them showed enough volume, any news could make their price jump, higher or lower, demanding too much attention. However, I was entering daily transactions on QQQ, the index composed of the one hundred largest companies of the Nasdaq market.

Many large Internet and technology companies were included in it and it was easily tradable with its large volume and significant liquidity. It was therefore an instrument of choice.

All markets had become quite volatile and the formulas of my strategies achieved good results. I quickly regained confidence, making profits gradually.

In March, the announcement of a stock split on QQQ, two for one, had raised its value to $221.63, representing $110.81 once divided, while double the amount of shares originally acquired by shareholders were owned by them. But when the euphoria of the stock split had evaporated, the index value fell by 40%, to reach a low of $72.25 in May, down by five waves.

For a while I had told anyone who would listen that the internet and technology companies would lose much of their value and I believed the index would come down. Nevertheless, it was a shame to have become convinced of that far too early and my colleagues who did not share my opinion had been right up to that time.

But even after the loss of the Nasdaq, many traders of the firm were still convinced the excitement and euphoria would return to a seemingly indestructible market, and they trusted that this unexpected reversal was only temporary.

As for me, according to my analysis, I regularly sold QQQ down in day-trading. This allowed me to get in and out fast, while leveraging funds to earn more profits, which piled up on each other. Indeed, because of sudden movements, I did not keep my positions overnight. I was content to make my sales every day, only when the price was negative, with a stop placed just at the level where the value would turn positive. That way, I was only short in a down market.

The drops and climbs were terribly violent and certainly not for the faint of heart. The behavior of the Nasdaq had surprised many and unfortunately, some of the operators got trapped and lost very large sums on shares that had collapsed dramatically.

I learned that one trader of another city's branch, a young man recently father of a little boy, had committed suicide by jumping out the window of his apartment. Although I did not know him, I felt awfully sad.

This job could be fatal, literally!

After two spectacular months of collapse, the index QQQ began to rise. The total down move between March and May was over 48 points; 61.8% of it represented a rise to $102. Using a psychological principle discovered by Ralph Nelson Elliott, an advance was to be five waves and a regression, only three.

However, unlike the pattern of an uptrend, which was only two steps back with a small recoup between them, this movement had more waves. Instead of falling by one-two-three between $110 and $72, there were two more waves which appeared to make a five, indicating the move as a major impulse on the descent.

I was expecting a serious change in trend and I wanted to prepare myself to profit from it. This downward movement allowed me to calculate my entry level for a longer-term strategy. I measured the potential retracement, from the top to the bottom of the large downward move in price and I added my Fibonacci retracements. Thus, I could estimate where I should sell short with greater certainty.

In September 2000, after a rise in just three waves, when the price attained what I called the BOX, which was a retracement up to 61.8% ($102), I sold short the index of the largest companies of the Nasdaq.

This time it was not a day-trade.

If the index was going to continue to rise, it would go over the last visible top, to make a higher high, which would prove that I was wrong. My entry was therefore at the area between 50% and 61.8% of the initial downward movement, at the end of a bounce in 1-2-3, from the low.

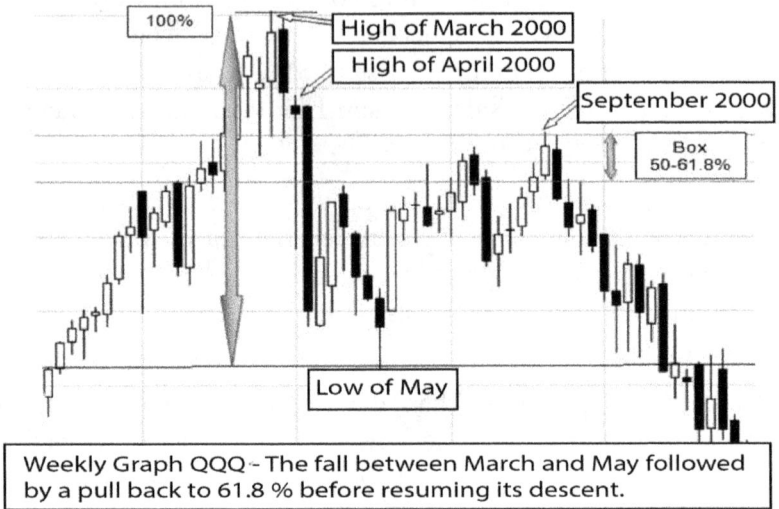

Weekly Graph QQQ - The fall between March and May followed by a pull back to 61.8 % before resuming its descent.

Fig - Nasdaq-QQQ

I was fairly confident of the resumption of the bearish trend and, to take into account the frightening volatility of the index, I placed my stop loss with good measure, just above the high of April. The first wave down had been followed by a violent rise back that same week, but that bounce back was largely erased by an even more dramatic descent, as the QQQ showed blatantly a much higher velocity when heading down.

Later on, as soon as the May low was broken, I changed the place of my stop, to put it just above the ceiling of September, reducing my risk to almost nothing.

With this practice of trying to let my trades continue while their stop was at breakeven, or close to it, I kept my position for several months, only changing my stops when I found a new strategic level.

Therefore, I had a free mind to trade other instruments.

Each time I wanted to enter a trade in a very volatile market, such as the Nasdaq during the summer of the new millennium, I was waiting for the price to come back to a zone between 50 and 61.8% of a sharp fall (the BOX). For explosions higher, I simply did the opposite and waited for a retracement of the same percentage to buy.

This long-term position, anticipating on the fall of the QQQ index was excellent and so my yearly results for 2000 ended largely positive, erasing my losses on Enron which were recovered and replaced with solid profits.

However, I had learned my lesson.

9/11/2001

High towers fall with a heavier crash;
And the lightning strikes the highest mountain.

—Horace

Since the release of my position focusing on gold in autumn 1999, I followed the price of the precious metal closely. After an advance of more than twenty percent in one day, the price had come down slowly over the next eighteen months. The velocity of the upward momentum had been impressive and the retracement to remove the entire advance was being done with a decreased volume and taking a very long time. This behavior gave me enough confidence in the recovery of its value.

My hypothesis respected the principle that a gap in price should be filled. I also considered the velocity of an instrument's surge. If the surge was followed by a slow decline back to the start of its move over a long period, the price would likely resume the first ascent in the original direction, as soon as the empty space was closed. So I invested in the precious metal for the long term. Futures being an early indication of the price to come later, the approximate value equaling $252 in 1999 was set at $265 in 2001.

To this position, I added silver whose graph showed an almost similarly vertical velocity from the middle of 1997, but with no gap. The Viking Hedge Fund Portfolio being larger, I had to report to the authorities the size of these investments. They were important but my mental stop was not too far from my cost and I was disciplined.

My stop on gold was just below the bottom, which had occurred before the millennium and the one on silver just under the low marking the bottom of the last four years. My philosophy behind the precious metals was in perfect accord with my bear bets on equities indices, while providing a balance in my portfolio with long / short positions.

On Monday September 10, 2001 at the close of trading, I went to my sports club for my gym class, as it had become my habit, before a light evening meal. The children were in France where they were now studying at university and I was alone.

Nothing attractive was on television and I was looking in my library for an interesting book, only I had read them all, apart from one that had been given to me almost a year earlier. The subject seemed futile to me, and I had not yet had any strong wish to open it.

It was a pretty box containing a book, a large piece of paper to unfold and a pack of tarot cards. The manual explained how to arrange them, randomly selected, and to place them on the support which, once opened, showed their spot. And then, from the position of each of them, the interpretations were revealed in the manual that accompanied the cards.

I did not believe in such predictions, but since I had nothing else to do, I carried on. As the explanations were revealed, I imagined the story would become clear... but I could not understand much of the comments and I did not see how any of it could relate to me. Actually, if there were an omen, it was pretty confusing.

The last image of the series was to announce the final result, but it was a tower where people were throwing themselves out screaming, and I concluded I was wasting my time with cards that meant nothing. Thus, without worrying about it, I put the whole package away, before going to bed.

In the middle of the night, a terrible pain woke me up. I felt my womb tearing and I ached so much I thought I was going to die. Unable to make a sound, my throat tight and dry, it was impossible for me to ask for help on the phone. With much effort, I literally crawled to my bathroom to look for a pill against pain that my dentist had prescribed a few months earlier after removing a wisdom tooth. And then, with great difficulty, I swallowed the drug before getting back to bed, crying from the ordeal.

Finally stunned by the narcotic, I fell asleep and woke up late the next day... it was almost nine o'clock.

As usual, my first move was to the remote control to find out the news on CNN and see what was going on in the world.

"BREAKING NEWS -. World Trade Center Disaster"

An explosion had occurred and a plane had struck the North Tower.

I got up, washed and dressed in a hurry, and went to my office where the phones were dead, just like at home. A second plane had hit the south tower and soon, I had to leave the building, which had to be evacuated a few minutes later.

Thousands of people rushed to get to Central Park and, since my apartment faced it, I had to head in that direction with the crowd. People were running, afraid that other buildings would crumble, the safest place seeming to be where there were no buildings over a large area.

In Paris, my children and my parents were probably worried but I had no way to reassure them. My attempts to call France and to tell them that the horrible disaster did not put my life in danger were in vain; it was impossible to have any phone communication and even less, an international line.

I had never worked at the World Trade Center. Since my internship in one of the upper floors of the twin towers in my early career, I went there only rarely. When I worked with Mr. Townsend I was not far away, but my trading desk had been for a long time in a skyscraper in midtown Manhattan.

In retrospect the explosion in the garage of one of the towers in 1993 had disturbed me more than I had realized. With hindsight, it was perhaps a premonition that had made me want to work elsewhere.

The whole world was shocked and terribly sad.

I knew several people who perished that day and I was extremely grieved. Suddenly, I realized that my race towards ever greater success took away from reality and that the welfare of human beings was more important than money. Following this event, as dramatic as it was unexpected, I realized that I had lost the sense of what was happening around me. Until then, I was only concerned for my family and how to understand markets…

But after this tragedy, I felt the need to have my feet on the ground and to be associated with the real existence, the life that people live outside investments. I was not too proud to ignore the suffering of others and, spontaneously, I decided to volunteer once a week at the Roosevelt Hospital, located on Fifty-ninth Street.

The lady in charge of the volunteering gave me a job to help patients with large disabilities every Wednesday afternoon, from 4 p.m. to dinnertime. I offered to teach arts and crafts classes, for them to do manual work, so they could use the movement of their fingers and hands, to build things for fun or create cards for their family.

With these occupations, they would do exercises to improve their motor skills, while being interested. Thus, for all the years following this dreadful day of September 11, and as long as I lived in New York, I never failed to give my time each week to the disabled and seriously ill of the hospital's third floor.

Later, when people asked me how I lived through the horror of 9/11, I spoke of my suffering from the night before and the card game which I did not understand at the time, but which had predicted the coming disaster.

One of my investors made the assumption that I might have a gift and that the vision of the card representing a tower from which people were throwing themselves out screaming, affected my subconscious mind and got me so upset that I became terribly sick during my sleep.

If that was a possible hypothesis, it seemed unbelievable to me!

OPTIONS

Since the beginning of my career as a trader and then as manager, I had avoided trading options and refrained from investing using some capabilities offered by the derivatives to hedge a portfolio of shares or to increase profitability at a "reasonable cost."

While some of my friends lived from options (those who benefited the most made a market in them) and while their conversations were filled with "butterfly spreads" and "iron condor" I really found no interest in them.

My office colleagues had sometimes called me "Miss all or nothing" and actually, if I thought a stock was worth it, I would buy it fully and directly, without further protection than my stop, mentally placed in a strategic location on the graph.

Although thousands of traders used options, and alternative portfolios adopted strategies very widely based on them, I really had no affinity for the methods to which they belonged.

The derivatives were often used and had their place in the operations of hedge funds, but I preferred to focus on what I knew well and what I could do better. Like any other specialty, a trader had to become an expert to do it profitably.

These instruments were classified in three different ways. "In the money" meant that if the option expired today, it would make money, "Out of the money" meant that it had gained nothing yet and "At the money" meant that the current price of the reference value was equal to the value of the "strike price" or elected derivative price.

You had to have a perfect knowledge of the "Greeks" or Greek letters, which were the names given to the way to evaluate the options.

For example, Delta was the ratio comparing the change in price of an asset to the corresponding price of a derivative, measured in Gamma, and Vega represented the option's sensitivity to changes in the volatility of the underlying instrument, it changed when large price movements occurred and fell as the contract got close to expiration, Theta established the rate of decline of the value of an option relative to the passage of time, and Rho was the rate at which the price of the derivative changed relative to the change of the risk-free rate of interest.

In a conservative portfolio, it was common to sell (write) a call option for every 100 shares the portfolio contained long (had been purchased). This strategy allowed the trader to receive a premium, obtained by the sale, while continuing to enjoy the rights to vote and also to receive dividends reserved to the owners of those shares. If the value did not rise too quickly, it enabled the trader to earn some extra money, received from such sales.

However, the benefit was limited because in exchange for the premium received from the sale of Calls, the trader could not fully benefit from the rise in value of these securities. If the stock had climbed above the price of the contract (strike price), it was mandatory to tender the shares at the agreed value, even if their worth had soared much higher.

Also, if an investor became negative on the market, he could buy put options, which were a kind of insurance policy to minimize losses. If the market turned seriously bearish, the option values increased in tandem with the fall, and profits were recorded on the latter, offsetting losses in long positions.

Apart from these basic uses, there were all sorts of combinations using options, but I always found the fees too high, compared to the profit potential.

In general, I avoided derivatives simply from personal choice. Why keep an investment and buy insurance that is relatively expensive, when it was just as well to get out of it, if one expected it to lose value?

Just as I considered it cumbersome to have too many tools on my charts, options strategies were further complications. Although I was probably capable of exercising the speed of the mind and thoughts cogitation, they moved away from my philosophy KISS (Keep It Simple Stupid).

The ultimate goal being to make money, why torture yourself with more difficult approaches that would fog up the process?

Yet from time to time, I had considered the possibility of using them, but each time, the total cost of options was too high to consider them really attractive and the risk-return to sell "Covered Calls" did not seem so positive, especially with the fact that these additional positions would be a distraction to my attention.

As for alternative strategies with options, in my opinion they were for those who did not have as strong an opinion as I had before making a decision and, frankly, they cost too much for their results, unless a rare opportunity arose that allowed the trader to draw the winning number. These instruments seemed reserved for traders who did not have enough capital to bet directly on investments.

Since my portfolio was large enough to do so, I greatly preferred to have, on the one hand, a list of short transactions with securities in an established downtrend and, on the other, a list with long positions that were going up and were considered the best on Wall Street. As such, I kept a long / short portfolio.

The weight of long to short positions depended on the behavior of the general market and the industry to which they belonged, of course.

Over the years, my refusal to trade derivatives was often criticized, especially since my only attempt to buy an option, when I had purchased the gold calls, was crowned with extraordinary success. However, even if I had really hit the nail with the options I acquired, I had been very lucky and I was conscious of it. Besides, my position had initially lost 60% of its value in two months, before seeing the price taking off like a rocket in one day.

Anyway, as a rule, I preferred to avoid trading options in my portfolio.

As 2002 began, the S&P500 index was still in an overall negative trend. Despite this, during the third quarter of 2001, the market had retraced part of the last movement down and went back up 61.8% to the "BOX."

It was at this level that I invested a large part of my portfolio, positioning it for the resumption of the downtrend. Since I anticipated a general decline, I added to my securities sold short, a position short also on the SP futures, to take advantage of the weakness to come. My stop for the S&P500 was just above the last high, established in January.

On the other hand, in addition to being long precious metals, I needed a few long positions in equities to balance a little bit my portfolio. The pharmaceutical sector being less likely to lose value than technology companies, I considered of course the various companies to buy.

While other big names shares were more popular, I was interested in American Home Product.

The company had signed an agreement for the purchase of Warner Lambert in 1999 and, at the last minute, had been supplanted by Pfizer, who had won the acquisition by a hostile bid. In compensation, AHP received the highest amount paid in history for this kind of "abandonment", amounting to a billion and eight hundred million.

So, while I bought the securities of the largest pharmaceutical conglomerates, I wanted to put an emphasis on AHP, which seemed to have good new products and, in the future, could moreover be the ideal candidate to also be absorbed by Pfizer.[4]

With the experience of my options on gold, more than two years before, and succumbing to criticism of not getting involved in

---

4 Seven years later, in 2009, Pfizer acquired AHP, which had resumed its former name of Wyeth.

options, I bought Calls for a quarter of a million dollars of American Home Product, while I was acquiring the shares of Merck (MRK) and Johnson & Johnson (JNJ) directly.

Of course, my options lost some of their value immediately, while the positions I had taken on other companies in the sector remained stable and even went up in price over the next two months.

Like any option to purchase, it was a bit like a coin toss. Again, I made a casino bet voluntarily arrogant; I knew I would pay dearly! And so indeed, my Calls on AHP expired worthless and I lost the quarter of a million dollars invested. I swallowed the cost of my loss on options with the feeling that I had deserved it, and I wrote in my diary that with this experience, the derivatives lesson was learned once and for all.

And then, when the market showed signs of weakening again, I got out of my other longs, which were mostly profitable. According to the market conditions and as the general trend was down, I decided that it would be safer to buy only with day-trades.

From now on, I would stay away from this kind of gambling and leave the trading of options to experts! As always, the best way to learn not to do something, was to lose money.

Smooth Sailing

If one does not know to which port one is sailing, no wind is favorable.

—Lucius Annaeus Seneca

As the years went by, I tried to have a steady income, while I was always on the lookout to discover a transaction for the long term that would be as profitable as gold.

The period between 2001 and 2003 was difficult. The markets were extremely volatile, with a much faster velocity in descents than in price climbs.

Therefore, I had to be especially careful not to be trapped with positions that could behave unexpectedly. My portfolio had to produce profits, whatever the surrounding issues.

To do this, I established my trading plan every day, regardless of the length of time that I would keep holding on to each investment. I always kept a portion of the money in cash in order to use it for my day-trading transactions, particularly when the market was unpredictable. This prevented me from taking the risk of an unexpected overnight event, and from getting the surprise of seeing one of my positions rolling over and lose the next day, not to mention that my profits accumulated more rapidly as I was constantly reusing the same capital for quick gains.

I kept remembering the advice of Bernard Madoff, which was to "parlay" the money and I applied it regularly.

However, the largest percentage of my assets were positions held over several weeks with a long / short balance. During the periods when the trend was downward, my short positions were in greater number, and in the times when the market resumed upward, the number of my purchases increased to tip up my portfolio towards the anticipation of a rise. From the beginning of 2003, the enthusiasm seemed to have returned to the markets and the sailing was in calmer waters.

According to the monthly chart of the SP500, the rise between the low of the October 1987 crash and the top that happened in January 2000 was remarkable. The stock market advance had been quite regular, making the usual waves. But since then, there had been violent up and down moves, with the index now having gone down for three years, enough to retrace part of its prodigious 1350 points advance, down to the Box Fibonacci (between 50 and 61.8%).

So it was a buy signal for the longer term.

For any position taken, it was obviously preferable to trade in the market direction, resulting in an overall much better performance. Doing so, this period between 2003 and 2006 was excellent for my fund and, in fact, quite easy to manage.

My positions on gold and silver were very profitable and out of curiosity, I had the idea of visiting a gold mine in Johannesburg. Then, since I was in South Africa, I took some vacation to visit Cape Town and the Western Cape, followed by an extraordinary safari in the heart of the bush. I chose the Singita Sasakwa Lodge, a game reserve heaven in Kruger Park from where I brought back amazing pictures, like five lions eating a giraffe, a leopard on a limb two meters away from my jeep as well as others of elephants, rhinos and hippos.

The same year, I went to visit India and Nepal and I also brought back wonderful images, some of them from the Himalayas.

In 2004, I chose to visit New Zealand and Australia, via several islands of Polynesia, including Bora Bora which I found to be paradise on earth and later that year, I toured Europe, visiting several countries as well as Russia. I was not as good a photographer as my son Thierry, but I did my best to bring the picturesque memories to show my family.

The following year was remarkable and my portfolio earned so well with my long term trades that I decided to "sleep" on my laurels and I closed all my positions in early December to tour the world for a month. I enjoyed particularly Asia, with my visits to Japan, Singapore and Hong Kong, as well as to Vietnam and Cambodia. In China, I was most impressed by Shanghai, which seemed more modern than New York in some parts, and Beijing with Mao's tomb and the forbidden city. Instead of taking sightseeing tours, I had a chauffeured car allowing me to visit places less touristy and I discovered a secluded area on the Great Wall, bringing back amazing photos.

Each trip always passed through Paris where the children were getting their graduate degrees. My life seemed so much easier when I was disciplined and using my strategies according to the rules. Rewards were so nice that, if I was sometimes tempted to take too many risks, then it was enough to remind myself of the pleasure of discovering magical places, of living in a beautiful apartment and driving a sports car. These considerations always brought me back to my disciplined and ordered approach!

It was out of question now to lose what I had won. My discipline was strengthened, and my risk management was a priority over what any trade could earn.

The only thing I lacked to be immensely happy, was a husband.

REAL ESTATE MARKET

*There are two types of people: those who try to win
and those who try to win arguments. They are never the same.*

— *Nassim Nicholas Taleb*

My family was the reason of my more frequent visits to Paris and I had the immense joy of spending time with my boys. In my heart, they were little, in my mind they were teenagers and in reality, I was always surprised that they were indeed adults. My children were men.

In New York, I spent all my summer weekends in Southampton, Long Island, where I rented a villa near the sea which was located about two hours by car from my Manhattan apartment, without risking a speeding ticket. During the winter, I went to Florida, where I met my friends to play golf or tennis and in doing so, "recharge my batteries" in the sun. Taking a flight from La Guardia, on Friday around 5 p.m., I was able to arrive in time for dinner in Palm Beach and, after a good relaxation far from the markets, I returned home on Sunday evening.

I used to dress elegantly and I gave the impression of working for a fashion house instead of being a trader. When people met me, they were far from knowing my responsibilities and I was careful not to talk about my activities. When I was not in front of my screens and especially during the weekends, I wanted to be a woman like any other.

In early 2006, I was at an art opening in a South Beach gallery. An unknown man, probably eager to impress me, said he "flipped" apartments in the area, boasting he was making a fortune, thanks to the constantly rising real estate market.

My smile was replaced by a serious expression to tell him that I anticipated an imminent decline in values. As proof, it was enough to look at the number of construction cranes occupying the horizon of Downtown Miami, and I added that it would probably be prudent to sell his properties quickly, because when the euphoria is too high, the end is usually pretty close.

After a loud laugh, he criticized my suggestion and, with a mocking air, replied that he was not worried, and that I'd better talk about fashion since I had no clue about his business. Without another word, I smiled graciously and I turned back to my friends.

My analysis showed that real estate values would surely go down and in fact, I had just sold the apartment I bought for my son Thierry, on 57th Street in New York. After his university studies in Paris, he had returned to Manhattan and, to respect his independence and his young adult freedom, I bought him an apartment not far from mine. However, a year later, he chose to return to France to work.

Sure, I could have kept it as an investment, but my research had led me to believe I should get rid of it. Thereupon, a real estate market top was made a few weeks later and, in Florida, the fall was 50%.

At the same time, I met my Prince Charming.

David was born in Manhattan and had studied at Peddie, Denison, Princeton and Harvard. His main activity was to coach great business leaders how to speak in public, but in the last few years he had invested in buying properties that were renovated and embellished for resale.

Most recently, he had sold all his investment properties and moved to South Beach, settling in a building where I had an apartment too.

I was impressed to learn that he had been alarmed by how very easy it had been to sell his houses and by the enthusiasm of buyers. He had an instinct or premonition that the housing market would not go much further and that it was better only to keep primary residences.

He was right.

Our ideas were on the same wavelength and I was impressed by his philosophy, his knowledge on all subjects, his kindness, his intelligence and fluency.

In fairy tales a handsome young Prince Charming and an even younger and beautiful princess fall in love, get married and live happily ever after. But in real life, maturity, knowledge of the world and common interests are often a better foundation for a strong and happy marriage.

David and I had much in common, and we were soon deeply in love. Our fairytale wedding ceremony was celebrated in France with my sons and entire family.

GRAINS

In my work in general, although I was a good trader, my troubles were often due to an anticipation of change in trend direction, derived from studies that were not confirmed by technical analysis. My overall performance was good, but without the help of tools letting me know the right timing, I was often too early.

After several past investments paid dearly for not entering at the right moment, I knew that I should not commit significantly as long as my trading system did not give me the green light.

However one day, my cycles' analysis showed that grains were about to explode higher and once again, I was tempted to act and my patience was rather limited.

The problem was to find what would be the perfect location to enter positions for the longer term and, in the meantime, I established a few day trades in soybeans, wheat and corn, to test the market. In this way, I was trading the grains in order to feel their behavior, while imbuing myself with their particular development.

It seemed better to wait because I had no signal to enter the market dictated by technical analysis. Furthermore, my fundamental research gave no encouragement at all. A large grain harvest, of top quality was confirmed, which could bring down their value tirelessly.

But I couldn't help noticing that several cycles were joining. I was on the lookout for any information, but I had to be patient. Every day, I watched the weather of producing countries, and I learned to read graphs for the different precipitations to anticipate rain. I was partly expecting coming destructive temperatures, which would have pushed up prices, but nothing happened and, increasingly, my mind became obsessed with weather predictions.

My constant struggle was to have the patience to wait for a sign without succumbing to the fear that I would miss a market upward move, and enter too early. My belief that there was a position to be had in agriculture was hard to tame.

The fact that the dollar had started a serious descent increased my conviction. Since the commodities were listed in dollars, a drop in the price of the US currency should, in principle, push up their value. Grains had gone higher already and, encouraged by this evidence, I accumulated hundreds of futures contracts, although this decision was only out of my cycles analysis and nothing technical was yet confirming my decision.

Joking with my colleagues, I imagined what the total amount of bushels in my position could represent, if they were delivered to me. According to my calculations, they would be the size of an entire block of buildings of the city of New York.

However, towards the middle of 2006, the grains gave back their lead and my confidence waned. I began to record losses and to doubt my previous arguments. Their unexpected behavior, which did not meet my expectations, while the dollar still declined, got me upset enough to lose sleep over it.

Naturally, my thoughts were conflicting and, on a Friday, feeling discouraged, I decided to exit my position to take a few days break. I had to rest, at least to get my thinking straight.

But then, the following Monday, the price of grain showed an up gap.

With commodities, this was rather common, but my bad timing gave me nausea. Within a few days, finally my system showed a strong buy signal. Obviously, if I had waited before establishing my first position, I'd probably have saved myself a lot of trouble. I was frustrated and, again, repentant. One thing was certain; it was imperative that I regained my discipline and respected my technical analysis. I wondered bitterly why, while I was a professional trader, I still made mistakes.

Without further ado, I bought back my position on all my futures grain contracts, with a stop mentally placed just below the last low in price and, this time I took advantage of their amazing move upward.

The meteoric rise darted with an almost vertical velocity and later, towards the end of 2006, I sold my contracts to record great profits. Subsequently, in early 2007, corn and wheat gave back some of their advance, while soybeans continued their momentum, just to regain more strength to run and double or even triple in value, but without me. While they came to a retracement level I was familiar with, such dramatic and irrational advances did not attract me. The risks were too clear and too damaging and I was not quite the daredevil I used to be, to participate in a climb that intense.

It was, however, just spectacular!

I had certainly grown older, but I felt unable to remain placid while facing such volatility and I shared the view of Sir Isaac Newton, lamenting over three centuries earlier:

"I can measure the movements of the body, but I cannot measure human folly."

Noting the remarkable new move forward, in which I only participated from time to time through day trades, I tipped my hat to those who had remained in the game.

The lesson I learned was that cycles analysis should always be added to Technical Analysis!

Market Top

I believe the very best money is made at the market turns.

—Paul Tudor Jones

Before a market made a top, there was always a sort of groundwork and several indications that professionals began to feel.

Yet it was easy to be blinded by all the positive comments on television and by analysts that followed one another, while influencing each other. Nobody dared to go against the consensus of the majority, affirming the market was strong.

But, the same way I had felt an imminent decline in the Nasdaq at the end of 1999, while the index increased in a hurry, over seven years later this kind of uneasiness took a hold of me, when I was watching the markets.

I had the firm intuition that they were ready to come down.

However, strengthened by my previous lessons, I was waiting for a sign from my trading system and did not intend to make the same mistake of entering a position only on fundamental or cyclical reasons, without the confirmation of my technical tools, which still showed nothing.

On Sunday, October 14, 2007, I was watching football on my movie screen with David and his close friends, but the game did not interest me, so I walked into my home office. Like every weekend, I wondered when the market would finally give me a sell signal.

I was working more and more from Miami Beach, where a trading system was installed, as sophisticated as the one I had in New York.

My instinct had been telling me for several weeks that the markets were ripe to fall in earnest, but I was determined to be patient, one of the greatest qualities of a trader. I did not want to proceed without an agreement from my formulas.

So I sat in front of my screens and… Surprise!

My most powerful signal announced a ceiling, not only on the SP500, but also on the Nasdaq and the Dow Jones. I felt deep inside me the certainty that I had to act, and now, all the ingredients of my anticipation method said absolutely to go for it.

It was time!

In fact, it seemed so huge that I wondered how I would warn my friends, and those who were not invested in my fund. I thought of sending them a word of warning, but I did not want to give the impression that I was looking for their business and I preferred to alert them impersonally.

I felt particularly generous that day, and I wanted to share my conviction for the benefit of everyone.

Of course, I could have been wrong. I did not feel the need to work as hard as I used to and I was hoping to spend more time in Florida, planning seriously for an early retirement in the coming years. Already, for over two years, I had no longer accepted new investors' money and, in order for the portfolio capital to be more easily manageable, its profits were distributed at the end of each year, instead of being reinvested.

This sell signal was an opportunity to make a nice gesture and to make my research public, but I waited for the game's half time to discuss it with my guests.

One of them, with his MBA in finance from a major U.S. school, argued emphatically that the P / E (ratio of prices in relation to earnings) of the SP500 was still relatively low, that its potential rise in value was excellent and as such, he strongly believed that I was wrong.

Smiling, I thanked him politely for his assessment, and turned to David who looked at the draft of what I was going to write and encouraged me, without hesitation, to make an official warning about the market top.

Letter to investors
From: Ninette Denise Uzan [mailto:nduzan@viking-fund.com]
Sent: Sunday, October 14, 2007 4:46 PM
To: ALL
Subject: ALERT-Stock market TOP
Importance: High

Throughout my career, I had the perilous responsibility of predicting the direction of different markets globally. This has been achieved primarily through macroeconomic and fundamental research, all the while considering investor sentiment.

But as Lord Maynard Keynes insightfully noted "Markets may remain illogical longer that we may remain solvent" – I include technical analysis to validate my work, a precious key in determining market timing.

These hard won insights into equities, currencies and commodities have been exclusively available to my private investors and attentive friends.

As of Friday October 12ᵗʰ, 2007, I am alerting everyone on my address list, of a MARKET TOP.

Since the probability is extremely high (>85%) that my technical system is right, while my macro and fundamental studies are flashing an overbought and irrational market, I feel compelled to tell you of an impending reversal in the stock market.

While most of my recognition came from buying gold back in 1999 or Corn and wheat in 2006, some of you may recall my dire warnings of the Nasdaq top shortly before March of 2000, and my bearish Real Estate forecast in the summer of 2005, and what followed.

My system had a sell on the Nasdaq on March 24ᵗʰ, 2000 and on the SP 500 cash on September 1ˢᵗ, 2000.

As of Friday, both the SP 500 cash and the Dow Jones Industrial index are showing historically similar SELL signals.

What this means to you is, you should get out of the stock market entirely, NOW.

Unless you buy enough puts to cover the entire value of your portfolio – and that costs money – you will not be safe. Do not take into consideration the capital gains tax you might incur, and don't get fooled by the FED's latest intervention, just get out and preserve your capital.

My advice is free - consider it as a generous gift... (Though potentially priceless, this is worthless if not acted on).

You might not remember me, or me you, but your email was in my address book, that makes you the beneficiary of my alert.

However, please do not call me for explanation, even though my retirement is scheduled soon, my time and attention is still fully committed to managing my fund and partnerships.

With the hope this will save you money and anguish,
Sincerely,
Ninette Denise Uzan

So, to all email addresses stored on my computer, I sent my message of recommendation to exit the market immediately.

The next day, I received some friendly responses from traders I knew, and a couple of messages with insults from people who were totally unknown to me, who had probably received my email through an intermediary... No matter.

The markets had indeed reached their top and dramatic events now unfolded, with most markets of the world starting their descent for a general decline of about 50%.

Thereafter my investors, traders, and many of my friends sent notes congratulating me and I was delighted to receive a multitude of thanks.

Some time later, a director of Bank BNP Paribas in Paris, Mr. C. du B., sent an email replying to my alarm, with simply:

"Thank you, a million times!"

Nothing could have given me greater pleasure. My intention to send an alert had been to help others and my goal reached its target.

Occasionally, during the terrible bear market that followed, I happened to share my perspective on the markets with some traders. My point of view differed sometimes from theirs, but our respect was mutual and it was always interesting to listen to the opinion of another professional.

Unlike the others, Mr. Art did not share his impression. He specialized in the trading of options and he called, from time to time, to know my feelings about the behavior of certain securities.

In December, at the end of the extremely bearish year 2008, where indices had lost almost half their value, the SP500 had turned sharply upward and it seemed that, finally, a floor was established in the market.

The first weekend of January 2009, Mr. Art asked me what I thought, but my response was not as positive as he had hoped:

"I could be wrong, but I think we are in the fourth wave and the fifth wave is coming. Normally, it should go below the low of November 2008. Also, I hate to admit it, but I'm a little wary of the general enthusiasm. Although the likelihood of a last leg down is not really clear, that case remains a very strong possibility. I'd personally be cautious and I am not inclined to buy at this time."

I was talking about the Elliott Wave.

My comment to Mr. Art was just a guess. However, after one last blast upward a few days later, the market resumed its descent and went down to break the low of November 2008, as I had predicted.

Again, my analysis had deciphered the upcoming wave five precisely. I had used the Elliott theory successfully on many occasions, notably to analyze and confirm the reversal of the Nasdaq in 2000.

But truth be told, it was easy to make mistakes in this study and the waves seemed often subjective, leaving one to consider different interpretations. Even though my analysis had been correct, it could as equally have been wrong. This is why a stop was always placed to protect a position.

However, another surprise awaited me…

Having had a strong sell signal exactly at the top of the market in October 2007, my system gave me an opposite alert, a powerful buy signal on the weekly chart at the close of Friday, March 6, 2009… Once again, it was proven that the two essential skills of a trader should be patience and discipline.

To demonstrate these qualities, great mental strength was imperative. Even with years of experience, my mindset had sometimes weakened. In these moments, I would go back to being careless and denying the demands leading to success, ignoring the rules I should respect and acting impulsively… and every time my misbehavior and my stubbornness had cost me dearly.

Anyway, I still survived through two key features. First, after recording a failure, I knew how to take me by the hand fast enough to resume my good habits and also, I felt an insatiable need to learn, to improve my knowledge and sharpen my trading tools.

So, the three years taken to perfect my technical analysis system at the beginning of my career had paid off throughout it.

I had managed to take care of my children and raise them to become admirable men, esteemed and established. With my love for them, I had undertaken a race, seemingly impossible to win, but my efforts and their results gave credence to the well-known phrase:

"Impossible is not French!"

NOTES

*The ultimate authority must always rest with
the individual's own reason and critical analysis.*

—*Dalai Lama*

To trade the markets, technical analysis proved absolutely essential.

Simple evidence that fundamental analysis alone could not suffice (as I bitterly learned, with my life's biggest losses) was demonstrated by two examples of a similar decision on interest rates, whose responses were diametrically opposed:

- In December 2007, the Fed lowered the interest rate in the U.S. and the Dow *fell* 300 points.

- In January 2008, the Fed lowered the interest rate in the U.S. and the Dow Jones *rose* 200 points.

Just a few weeks apart, and a similar decision caused totally different results.

Since technical analysis was the study of the price, which itself was a demonstration of the emotions and the psychology of all market participants, its understanding was vital and had to be added to any other research, as corporate balance sheets and other reports were often misleading...

The examples were numerous.

Enron, Tyco, Qualcomm, Freddie Mac, Fannie Mae, these favorites of Wall Street, had long deceived investors. And then, on top of their glory, they suddenly lost their luster and had collapsed.

I had previously written the following paragraph, in a report published in June 2003, when I questioned the actions of a government agency:

The firing of the three top executives of the Freddie Mac Corporation is very puzzling. Their extensive derivatives activities are no secret - $700 billion as of last week. The scary part is that no one bothers to question how a company, dare I say a government agency, is being exposed to derivatives in an amount almost double the United States deficit for 2003, an amount growing to get close to 10% of GDP? Could there be a scandal brewing?

The value of a Freddie Mac (FRE) share was nearly $65 when I wrote my article. And then, after making a final top, just above $74 in late 2004, the price had fallen to be worth only pennies in 2008.

However, warning signs had appeared in their price chart several months before the fall of these securities!

Epilogue

If you want a happy ending, that depends, of course, on where you stop your story.

—*Orson Welles*

In the fall of 2009, my children had completed all their long studies and lived in Paris.

My eldest, Thierry, was director in a large IT company and married to Ethel, a young woman as intelligent as charming. To my great joy, they told me they were going to have a baby.

As for my younger son, Maxime had followed my example by choosing to work in finance where he started with a sales trader position at a large investment bank in Paris.

At first, when he was puzzled by the behavior of the New York Stock Exchange, I explained over the phone the logic behind these contradictory reactions, knowing that when I started, I had been confused myself. His passion for the markets had greatly facilitated the progress of his career and he was on the verge of becoming a portfolio manager in its own right.

In the near future, he was planning to marry his girlfriend Virginie, a pretty brunette equally as lovely as Ethel and I was delighted.

Increasingly, I regretted living so far from them, but I was proud of my sons and I was glad to know that they had chosen quality people for companions, girls with whom I felt an immediate affinity, and whom I loved just as much as if they were my own daughters.

Shortly after the birth of Madison, my granddaughter, I suffered from a very serious illness and had to close my fund, to the dismay of my investors. The doctors forbade me any stress and prescribed a complete rest. Overall, they were quite pessimistic and did not give much hope for recovery, despite the best treatments following my surgeries. Not knowing how long I would live, I decided to return to France to be closer to my family.

So, I left the United States after twenty-five years and moved to Paris while my dearest husband, attentive as always to my well-being, courageously adapted to a different lifestyle and a language he had to learn.

Fortunately, thanks to his attentive presence, ongoing care and the profound happiness I felt being surrounded by my children, my recovery was almost miraculous. But rest was still required and, since I was still forbidden to trade, I decided to write my first book to occupy myself.

My idea was to teach good manners to my little Madison, through a fairy tale. I thought it would be more fun for her to learn to behave like a real princess while listening to a good story.

And then, after many months, I regained some of my solid health and David surprised me by installing a trading platform in our apartment. He knew that my greatest pleasure was to follow the markets and that I had missed this activity.

I was thrilled!

With the time difference, I noticed it was very easy to make transactions on U.S. exchanges and apparently I had not lost my "golden touch". Futures and Forex were open almost continuously, and being in a different country did not change much. So I could make a trade from time to time without any fatigue or stress, because my positions were very tiny and only kept for a few minutes.

The particular advantage in trading from France was when the futures indexes or commodities had showed a nice move the day before, the price would retrace some of its advance to consolidate during the night, when it was morning in Paris.

This allowed me to enter at a better price, to benefit from the continuation of the trend established, without thereby being sleep-deprived. Being six hours later than Europe, the U.S. markets opened when it was mid-afternoon in Paris and, therefore, following the quotes turned out to be a pleasant pastime.

Once I completely regained my health, I was invited to a conference on hedge funds in a renowned business school.

Wearing a dark suit, a manly shirt and tie, like when I worked on Wall Street, I explained my job to the audience and answered their numerous questions. That day, I discovered the strong interest of the students in the profession of trader. This news was my inspiration to write again, in order to teach this study.

I intended to explain each tool with its benefits and how to interpret its information. But upon reflection, I only selected the most efficient in order to keep the explanation simple and not to complicate things. One of the lessons from my experience was to prefer quality instruments to their quantity. But it was imperative to give a special weight to the intellectual aspect of trading.

In describing my job, it seemed necessary to talk about the psychological strength to follow rules, since the mental work proved invaluable. In addition, my presentation of learning could only be effective if I revealed the essential mental traits to cultivate for this profession.

Throughout my career and even when I took enormous risks, my concern had always been to survive. More than anything, my efforts were to acquire a powerful self control and a keen knowledge, combined with a fierce discipline to do my trading job, while respecting the rules of a winning strategy.

This is why I had to emphasize the mind set required to succeed, as well as the importance of risk management.

So just like on the cover of my journal, where I drew the cornucopia supported by three pillars, the components of these criteria had to be included in an obvious way.

The first column was built with careful preparation, the use of proven tools and the accumulation of all the requirements listed in successful strategies.

The second was to assume a good risk management to avoid the disasters resulting in major losses. While these problems could happen in a short time, they required many weeks or even months of disciplined work to win back.

And the third, perhaps most vital, was made of the trader's intellectual power, showing a foolproof discipline.

Thus the size of the position, the respect for stops and the establishment of laddered exits, allowing the trader to reach a breakeven point securing the transaction, had to be part of the preparation and represented important trump cards to achieve success, by multiplying the chances of making money. Besides, my journey was proof. Each of the huge losses I had weathered was due to the refusal of one of these principles.

It was then that, as I had taught good manners with a tale to my granddaughter, I thought it would be better to reveal my profession with a story.

For a simple description of the tools that I used, I decided to tell my career and what I had learned. My path was not ordinary, but I managed to prosper and I had more than twenty years of experience. So I was able to provide evidence for all those who dream of becoming traders, that success is well within the reach of all.

Throughout the years, my insistence on discipline, the many affirmation sentences and the lists of rules to follow were probably repetitive, but they helped me to survive. Moreover, even having made blunders, my attention to dwelling on these details, allowed me to achieve the goals of my ambitions.

The message of this book takes the phrase written above the blackboard of my childhood classroom:

"If you want, you can… Become a trader!"

To get there, everyone must go through his own journey, being armed with great determination and continually seeking to find opportunities. Once you have trained your eyes to distinguish the possibilities, to focus your energy to seize them and to manage your head to comply with the rules, there will be no limit to the wealth of benefits that you can get.

I did my best to describe to you, in all humility and sometimes with a little embarrassment, how costly it is to be stubborn, undisciplined, and without preparation. Like me, you'll have to make your own mistakes and you will most likely try to reinvent the rules.

However, I do not recommend it. Instead, feel free to use the tools and strategies I used. They will help you. And then, keep a log of your activities where profits and losses are visible, but make sure your preparation, your risk management and flexibility are more obvious.

The story ends with the hope of encouraging those who wish to embrace this profession, to reassure those who doubt that success is possible and to remind everyone that patience and discipline are the essential qualities to stay the course.

This is not the end, it is the beginning of your experience ...

Some details of analyses follow.

With my best wishes for success in your trading and also in your life. Now, it's your turn to play!

Tools & Analyses

Technical Trading

Logic is the technique by which we add conviction to truth.

—Jean de la Bruyère

There are numerous books on technical analysis, detailing all kinds of candles, indicators and formations, and how to interpret their meaning. But to be profitable, the key is not how many instruments we use, it is how good they are and how well we use them.

The following analyses and tools are only those, in my opinion, which have proven to be simple, effective and efficient, in order to understand a chart. The goal is to make money, not to complicate things, following the KISS principle.

First and foremost, a trader looks closely at the different index quotes for indications about the market "internals" which analyze its health, check its temperature, and measure its pulse and its "breathing."

Just below the quotes of the Dow Jones and the S & P 500, is found the NYSE TICK index. It measures the number of shares executed on an uptick (a transaction higher, made on the offer after one on the bid) compared to the number of those executed on a downtick (a trade down on the bid, after one made on the offer). It measures this on all shares traded on the New York Stock Exchange. If the figure is approaching 1000 or even 1200, it is reporting an overheated market and a pull back down is imminent, for a short time intra-day. Conversely, a number of -1000 to -1200 witnesses a terribly bearish mood which can result in a snap back up, if only for a moment.

When the market is very strongly trending upward, the TICK level can reach 1,500. In this extreme case, it is interpreted as strong momentum, which insures a continuation in the direction of the trend. By contrast, if the market digests a powerful movement backwards, ticks indicate the end of the downturn. This information is useful if the trader wants to place a buy order in a bull market with a TICK level at about 1100, as he is advised to wait for a return to 800, before entering his long trade.

Then, the TIKI takes into account the upticks and downticks among the 30 stocks in the Dow Jones Industrial Average; a number over 24 is a remarkably strong level.

Next, the TRIN, also called "ARMS INDEX", is a trading tool used in technical analysis. Its formula is calculated as follows:

TRIN = (Number of advancing issues / number of declining issues) divided by (total volume of advancing issues / total volume decreasing issues).

A value of less than 1.00 is considered bullish and greater than 1.00, bearish. For example, in days of panic, like those of the violent crash of October 1987, the TRIN has been known to touch 5, but this is extreme. A major decline would normally touch 2.00 and the figure can be 0.50, if the market is up sharply.

However, it is mostly the direction and evolution of TRIN that are important. If the TRIN goes from 0.70 to 1.01, it indicates that the market is recording large numbers of sales and is going to head down rapidly.

Another index to consider is the VIX. The volatility index of the Chicago Board Options Exchange is designed to track the S & P futures, as an independent entity. Calculated on the basis of the options activity on that index, the VIX is used as an indicator of investor sentiment in general. High values are a sign of pessimism and low values means that optimism is high. It is an important reference and traders keep an eye on it, because any excess can announce an upcoming change.

The ADD, the Advanced-Decline line is also carefully watched. It shows the cumulative sum of the difference between the number of shares going up and the number of the ones declining in the market index. The level moves up when more shares are advancing relative to the number of those declining and it moves down when more securities are down than going up. This indicator can also be applied to the volume of the shares up to the volume of those down.

And then, of course, the graphs are analyzed. Each diagram is calculated from four data entries:

Open (O) - High (H) - Low (L) - Close (C), to which is added the volume (V), the latter appearing at the bottom of the chart, separately and away from the price bar showing the OHLC.

The Open is the first transaction of the day. The beginning of the day is rather influenced by individuals. It is often an emotional response that influences only part of the morning.

The Close marked by the last transaction is especially important to the professionals. Institutions buy and sell later in the morning and in the afternoon, usually after researching the facts. Their orders "market on close" are typically pretty indicative.

Some chart patterns do not need any analysis tools to be easily visible, like an inside day. If the bar or candle is within the range of the previous day, the following day tells the direction to enter a trade, as if the price goes higher than the inside day, it is a buy, and lower, it is a sell.

Obviously, if there has been a battle without a winner and neither buyers nor sellers can get the last word, the next day's price behavior shows which of the two groups still has ammunition. Thus, this struggle looks like a small indecision candle, in the middle of the previous day's price range.

If the price went below the trigger candle which was inside the range of the previous one, an order to sell was placed, and the stop level was just above the high of the inside candle.

If the price went above the small candle, a buy order was entered. Its stop placed just below it.

Inside day: The trigger candle is inside the previous one.

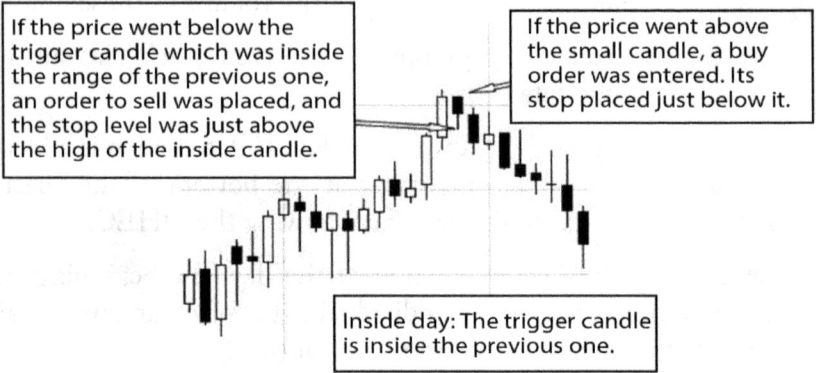

FIG - Inside Day

So the next day, a break of this price ambiguity, up or down, gives direction to enter a position.

Also, it is necessary to analyze a longer-term chart, to verify the trend, even if the trader only day-trades. For example, if trading on a five minutes interval, it is advisable to check if the trend also agrees with the direction visible, on both a 15 minutes and a one-hour chart. All insurance has to be taken so that the position shows the most potential to generate profits.

Another easy way to find trades without tools is to look for previous gaps in price, since they have a strong probability to get filled.

A gap in price is likely to be filled

FIG - Gap

The easiest way to look at the price history of an instrument is done by studying its price evolution on a graph. Charts can take on very different appearances.

Some of them only consider the day's closing price, which is indicated by a line. Those are rarely used and are reserved for markets with very low volume.

More informative, "Bar Charts" are shown as bars, called OHLC (Open - High - Low - Close), where each vertical line illustrates a price movement over the period considered. The small dash to the left represents the opening and the right dash, the closing. If the indent on the right is higher than the left, the instrument has closed up from the opening and, if lower, the close is down. These bars are sometimes colored in white or green for an increase and in black or red for a fall, so it is easier to show in which direction they are going. The price range of the bar is the High minus the Low (HL).

However, the vast majority of technical traders use candles, which provide more guidance.

Candlestick graphs date back to the 1700s, when Homma, a Japanese rice trader, discovered that price is influenced by human psychology, as well as by supply and demand. Homma amassed a great fortune using candlesticks; it is said that he never lost money using them.

A candle is recognized by the fat part, the candle's body, which is the difference between opening and closing. The price from the top of the range to the body leaves a line like the wick of a candle, giving its name, and from below its body to the low, is its shadow. As with bar graphs, upward candles appear in green or white, and downward candles, in red or black.

These candlesticks are not difficult to interpret and can be used in combination with all the traditional indicators. They reveal opportunities for trades, while helping to filter the data for better timing. They also warn the trader of the possibility of a change in trend. Their ease of use is based on the same principle as the OHLC Bar Charts. Their names are easy to remember; yet only a few seem essential, out of the many kinds.

They define the market momentum by the number of candles in the same direction (easily seen by the color) and their body accentuates the difference between the opening and closing, while their range is the total size of the candle. A long candle with a small wick and a short tail is very negative in black (or red) and very positive in white (or green). The shorter the price range, the more buyers and sellers clash, without either having the power to have the last word.

Often a small candle like this can indicate an impending rollover, since there is indecision and neither buyers nor sellers have been able to gain the lead.

Another figure, the Doji, proves significant.

It is formed when the opening and closing price are the same, thus forming a cross. The length of shadows above or below can vary, therefore giving a different interpretation.

A Doji reports, in general, the possibility of an ending of the established direction. When a Doji has no upper wick and the opening and closing are the same price and at the top of the range, with a long tail, it reports an upward trend since the buyers have won, although just after opening, sellers have tried to get the price down. Only in the end, the close is still at the highest. When such a structure, called Dragon-Fly, appears on a market floor, it is seen as a signal of a turn towards an upward trend.

However, the easiest and safest use of the Dragon-Fly is when it appears in a bullish trend. It proves its continuation and confirms it, since while the sellers have wanted to lower the price, it is in vain. The trend is too strong and the price has closed at its highest.

Its opposite, a wick with the opening and closing at the same price at the bottom end of the range, is called a Gravestone. With this ominous name, it signals the emergence of a new downward trend and, especially when viewed at a market top, it is interpreted as a change towards the downside. Buyers have tried to raise the price, but sellers have won and the value has closed at its lowest.

These Dojis have no body. With the other candles, however, the location of their trunk is decisive. A small upwardly body forming a hammer shape is positive, for example, while its opposite, a downwardly small body forming an inverted hammer is negative. Whether visible on short or long-term charts, candles give an easy reading; but candlesticks don't perform miracles.

Whatever their appearance and interpretation, it is important to understand that they show exactly the price movements, according to the transactions executed. From there, the trend is determined and from this trend, the projection of likely changes in price are made. Thanks to the historical database, the possibilities of future behavior can be calculated and analyzed. Traders follow certain rules to analyze candles and they often use the smaller ones in their formulas, predicting an end to a recent evolution.

FIG - Candlesticks

Of course, the higher the probabilities, the more likely the system is effective.

Strategies are considered in back-testing, taking care to note if the market is up or down. Considering the general behavior of the market, whether sleeping or on the contrary very volatile, entails the use of different strategies. Some systems perform best for a particular kind of price conduct, in which case the appropriate method has to be chosen according to the market environment.

There is another type of chart, called "Points & Figures" which is unique in that it does not take time into consideration, unlike all the other techniques, but only the price. It is sometimes used to confirm the trend and, more often, to capture an overall view of the value considered.

The chart looks like a game of Tic-Tac-Toe (or Noughts and Crosses), made with X and O, and is used to try to predict important levels over longer periods. Prices are recorded against the changes of direction, drawing a column of X for the increases and a column of

O for the declines. It is a way to check the trend and get buy and sell signals, compared to previous levels, without the need for a personal interpretation.

The graphs are constructed by first deciding what is the value represented by each X and each O. Most of the time this is set to 1x3, although it can be changed according to the needs of the trader. A column is altered only when the price changes direction by the value of a number of X or O.

Traditionally, the continuation of the rise in price is marked with an X for each point (or $1 per box), forming a bullish column. Three full points in the opposite direction are required to change the up column of X and move to a bearish column, this time made of O. Any change in prices below the value of the box is not considered, making the Points & Figures a kind of filter which ignores small changes in value.

Trends can be plotted, the best being at a 45 degrees angle. A trend break upward represents a buying signal, and one downward, to sell short.

45% Down trend - Breakout and ascent

FIG - Points & Figures

These graphs are generally used to obtain a general idea, regardless of the time required to affect the price, because they are very slow to signal a trend change.

Most traders therefore use candlesticks to analyze the charts and Points & Figures to confirm the general interpretation of their long-term conclusions.

VOLUME

Irony is just honesty with the volume cranked up.

—*George Saunders*

Any transaction is made by the agreement between a seller, who wants to get rid of his securities, and a buyer, who wishes to possess them, each trying to get the best possible price. The quantity exchanged at a certain level is therefore significant.

On the chart, volume is located below the price graph and separated from it.

More than any other indicator, the volume associated with the movement of an instrument is crucial. Traders always keep in sight the information it reveals, knowing that the size of the quantity executed underscores the change in value. The number of shares changing hands at that level justifies the value being higher, or condemns its weakness.

When the volume bar is tall and the price candle stays small, it is a warning signal. In this case participants have indeed been numerous and the orders are clearly magnified, but while the battle has been particularly severe, almost no advance or retreat is visible in price. It often heralds in a trend change.

By combining this indicator with the price, the evolution shows more meaning and lends weight to its worth or, on the contrary, proves questionable. An upward momentum, with double its volume compared to its average, means the impulse is stronger as the orders mass has increased.

Volume Bars can be linked to their high points to draw a trend, confirming or doubting the price direction. For example, if the value has risen over a time period while the trend of the high volume points are declining, the price increase is denied by the action of this indicator.

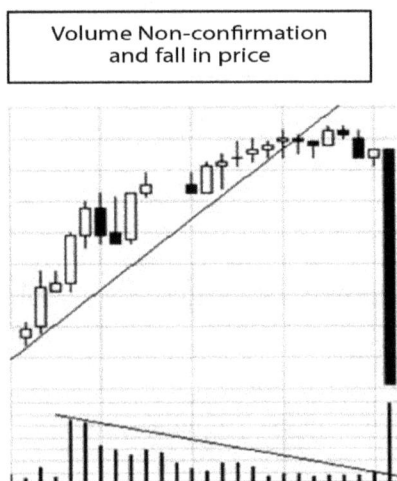

FIG - Volume

"Up on down volume" (rising prices accompanied by a decreasing volume) is a behavior traders are enormously wary about. In all cases, the volume measuring the extension of the value has a preponderant significance.

TREND

Efforts and courage are not enough without purpose and direction.

—*John F. Kennedy*

Normally, the indicators are supposed to give signals to buy or sell, but when traditionally viewed they often proceed with delay and achieve very poor results. However, if they are used to confirm or deny a market trend, they can perfectly anticipate the progression of the instrument analyzed. This feature makes them indispensable.

In general, the easiest way to use a trend is to follow it. A trade in compliance with the dominant evolution has a greater chance of success than one made without the support of the established inclination, or going against it. It is much more difficult to anticipate a trend reversal than to follow the prevailing price direction and to participate in its continuation.

A bullish trend is represented by higher highs and higher lows than the previous ones and, conversely, a downward trend is indicated by lower lows and lower highs.

Trading in the direction of a bull market is to buy after a retracement or "dip" in price, when the price then returns to its 20 periods moving average, after having moved away from it.

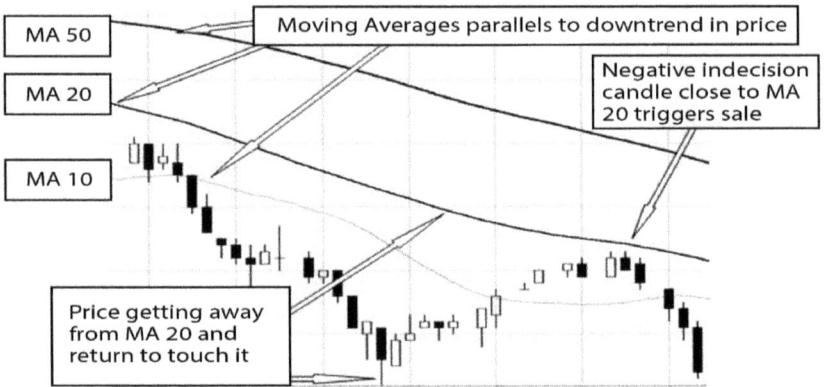

FIG - Trend trading

Conversely, in a bear market a sell is indicated when, after a sharp decline, the price has pulled back slightly to return and touch the area around the average line of 20 candles, while the moving averages of higher length are almost parallel, downhill.

Particularly when the price has gone too far down by a large distance from its MA20, it is advisable to wait for a retrogression back to touch it again.

Of course, one single reason is not sufficient to establish a trade. Several success probabilities have to be accumulated, along with different indicators regrouped at the same level, indicating the ideal point, while giving more weight to the entry decision. Also, these calculations are used to find out where the strategic place is to put the stop, to securely protect the position.

Trend lines can also be drawn, joining every high to locate the level of price resistance and lining all the lows to find the support level. The most consistent trend is at 45 degrees, its velocity being neither too fast nor too slow, just like in the Points and Figures graphs.

As long as the trend line is not broken, the direction of the price remains the same.

Two closes outside a trend line are required to indicate a change of direction, but it is rare that a market turns without a moment's hesitation, being characterized by one or several small candles indicating a period where neither buyers nor sellers have the last word.

However, it is possible that the trend line is just touched and exceeded by only one or two ticks, without really being canceled or removed. This does not mean anything, and therefore it is reasonable to give some comfort to the position with a stop placed at a price that would confirm this breakout.

In general, false breakouts are followed by a resumption in the initial direction, despite the very slight overshoot.

The end of a trend is often marked by a consolidation period, while the value draws a sort of bottoming or topping on the graph.

In particular, using the example of an uptrend, if the price descends low enough to break down the support line which has followed the price higher, the possibility of a reversal is considered. Any long transaction is exited automatically, since the stop is found just under this support. In this case, to take advantage of a shift lower, the trader has to wait until the price goes back to touch the trend line from below, to establish a short position that is betting, this time, on lower prices. A protective stop is placed over the last high, which occurred before the break.

This strategy assumes that a trend line that has been a support, becomes resistance once the support line is broken. In trading, this is a golden rule:

"Once broken, support becomes resistance and vice versa."

A previous support becomes an obstacle, establishing a solid ceiling and stopping the price from going above it. That is why a protective stop is placed above this level.

Although not likely, it is possible that the price will turn back up to continue the initial upward trend, but in that case, the stop is hit at new high, and the risks remain small.

Inversely, when a value shows an established downward trend, a price move above the line joining all the downward trending highs and breaking the line to the upside will automatically terminate the short position, since a protective stop is in place just above that resistance line.

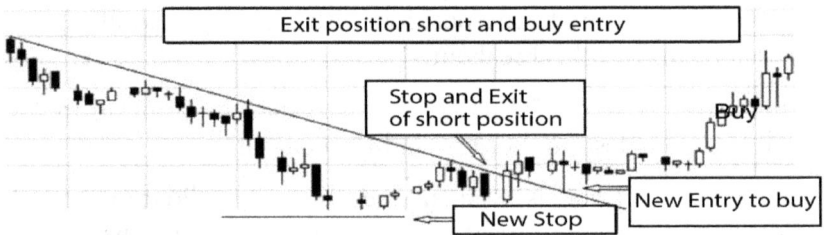

FIG - Trend Reversal

As before, but in the opposite direction, if the price comes back down and is stopped by that line, previously a line of resistance but acting now as support, this is an indication that the trend has turned upwards and therefore, the trader is encouraged to buy. As a precaution, a stop is placed below the last low, just for the remote possibility that the price will break the new support and resume its descent with a new leg down.

Breakouts offer excellent opportunities but, once again, patience is advised because the price often returns to test the trend line in the other direction. It is therefore better to use this setback as an entry point, which has a better chance to result in profits.

Simply put, since the transactions anticipating a turnaround prove to be more risky, it is recommended to go with the flow and exit the position when the trend line is broken.

When the new direction becomes clear, it is easier to trade along.

MOVING AVERAGES

A moving average shows the average closing price of an instrument over a fixed term. The risks are inherent to the moving average's length of time. A moving average covering a short period is a fast moving average and is sensitive to price changes. A moving average covering a longer period and calculating many bars is slower. As a general rule, the slower the speed, the less reliable it is. The main use of a moving average is to confirm a trend and to support its direction. When several lines of different periods are leaning, in the order of their size, in parallel to the price trend, they substantiate its route. They can be simple (SMA), adding the price of each close and dividing their sum by their number (MA20=total divided by 20) or exponential (EMA), applying more weight to recent prices.

These indicators are used in several ways.

The first concept is simple: the trader buys when the bar closing price is above the chosen moving average and he sells when the close falls below it. This strategy is profitable in a trending market (up or down), although not recommended during periods of consolidation or "sideways market." Some traders see a slow moving average as an indicator to stay in a buy position for the longer term, as long as the price remains above the average and as a sign to get out, if the price goes below.

The second use takes two moving averages, one fast and one slow, to establish a trade if they cross. This feature gives a signal to buy if the fast moving average crosses the slow one from below upwards, and conversely, to sell if the fast, coming from above and moving down, passes the slow.

Death Cross

The Death Cross is visible on SP500 on 12/26/2007 (daily chart) at 1497.66 and a Golden Cross formed on 6/25/2009 at 920.26. These signals alerted of most of the fall and the recovery.

FIG - Death Cross

Moving averages can act as support or resistance lines, stopping the price from passing through them. The longer periods moving averages are quite lethargic and very easy to detect, while their crossing can be really impressive. Some of them are notorious.

A "Death Cross" is when the 50-day moving average comes from above in a downward direction to cross over the 200-day average. This is a signal to sell a market for the longer term.

Its opposite, the "Golden Cross" is simply the reverse. When the MA50 comes from below and crosses up above the MA200, the Golden Cross is a call for major acquisition.

With three moving averages using 10, 20 and 50 bars, a buy signal is given when the MA20 crosses the MA50 upwards, while the MA10 is already over it.

A sell signal is indicated when MA20 passes MA50 coming down from the top, while MA10 is already below. The most frequently consulted are the 20 - 50 - 100 and 200 moving averages and their most important intersections are 20/100 and 50/200.

However, these crosses are not infallible. The weakness of moving averages is inevitably that they have a time lag relative to the market and that their intersection does not necessarily forecast a change in trend; they have to be used otherwise.

It seems best only to consider them as a confirmation of the trend continuation, and a demonstration of its leadership, visible by the fact that they are located in parallel to the price.

As such, the easiest and most effective use of moving averages to make money is in a well-established trend with the MA lines moving parallel to the trend. When the price has then gone too far away from the area surrounding the MA20, the strategy is to wait for the value to retrace back to touch it with low volume. The entry is made, provided that a small indecision candle (negative for a downtrend and positive for an uptrend) signals the end of the retracement.

Small negative candle (downtrend) on MA 20

A small hesitation candle signals the end of the upward pull back at the touch of MA20, indicating to sell short before a resumption of the downtrend.

FIG - Trend following strategy

It is dangerous to establish a position if the entry price is too far away from the MA20 line. The return of the price to that equilibrium would be a safer entry to trade, in anticipation that the value of the instrument will continue in the direction of the established trend after this regression. The small trigger candle signals the fight between buyers and sellers and hints at the end of the retracement.

In a downtrend, if the price is lower than the bottom of the candle of uncertainty, it is a sell signal, and the stop is just above its high, the risk being minimized. Obviously, in the case of an uptrend, the opposite is true.

This strategy is very effective, especially since all lines of longer durations are parallel to the price and follow the trend.

This way of using moving averages is more profitable than employing crosses, and good operators use this strategy regularly.

Support - Resistance

When trend lines are placed in parallel, the lower marking a floor price when buying interest is renewed and the higher a price ceiling where sellers become more aggressive, they form a channel.

These lines are extensions points that join all the highs and all the lows in price for a period, and they allow the trader to identify the support and resistance.

Support is the bottom of a trend and resistance is its top, so it is recommended to buy near the support on an uptrend and to sell near its resistance, a strategy called fading trend.

In the opposite direction and to follow a downward trend, the strategy is to sell short near the resistance and cover (close) the position near the bottom, as long as the price remains confined in the channel.

The principle here is to wait for a market to be overvalued and therefore, when buyers are visibly exhausted or have disappeared, to decide to sell as the price has reached a level of resistance and avoid being in while the price returns down to its equilibrium.

In contrast, when the price is undervalued and sellers come to be exhausted, it is time to buy.

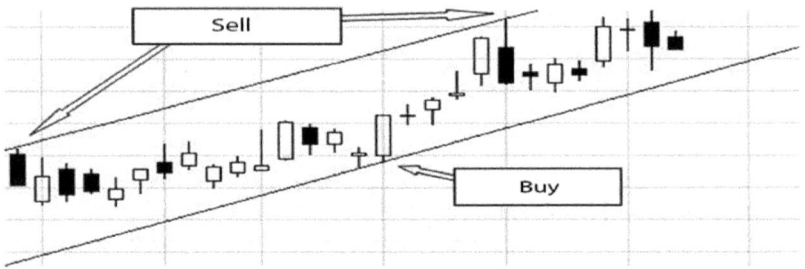

FIG - Channel

At a certain level, sellers are more likely to return and the value falls until it reaches such a low cost that buyers finally take over and the price comes back up.

Sometimes in consolidation periods, when the trend lines are lateral, the price can pass through this line while its close is still inside the channel. In this case, it does not count.

The fundamental rule about support and resistance is considered a golden trading rule. In principle, a broken support becomes a resistance or ceiling, which prevents the price from passing through and climbing back higher, and a resistance transforms into support, halting the price decline by a floor, preventing it from going lower.

These price levels are even more significant if they are horizontal. They show the level (support) at which buyers are willing to grab the instrument and enter the market, and the top (resistance), where sellers are willing to get rid of it.

It is at these levels that the chart experiences tension to bounce back, or pressure to fall.

Also, in a strong uptrend, when the price tries to go higher, and its several attempts are stopped by a horizontal line of resistance, while the candles are becoming smaller and regrouping below that line, a breakout upward of this powerful level is even more important.

Breaking the resistance often comes with a greater force since the pressure has been rising for a while.

As such, a trade can be entered in advance just above the seemingly unbreakable resistance, which, if the price does go through, will generate a quick and easy trade.

> **Buy just above the flat resistance level to anticipate a continuation of bullish trend**

> **Stop just below the last higher low**

FIG - Momentum Breakout

The Momentum Breakout strategy takes advantage of the often fierce movement, allowing for rapid and substantial profits.

For this trade, the purchase order is entered in advance just above the resistance line acting as ceiling and, since the basic hypothesis to enter the trade is that the uptrend will continue, making higher highs and higher lows, the protective stop is just under the last low, which, if touched, will make a lower low in price and will deny the uptrend supposition.

On the other hand, this principle is equally valid in an established downtrend, when the breakout of a very solid support will reward a short position entry, just below its line.

Support and resistance are excellent indicators and are important tools in the study of technical analysis.

INDICATORS

Vagueness is at times an indication of nearness to a perfect truth.

—*Charles Ives*

The most basic trading principle is simply to follow the trend (Trend-Following). However, only one criterion is not sufficient to ensure a successful transaction.

A trader needs to have accumulated the greatest possible probabilities of success, and it is necessary to add a number of pieces of evidence to give more weight to a signal of resumption of the trend after a pull back.

One of the criteria is to consider the indications around the pivot points, often acting as resistance or as support. These points are determined before the opening of the market and, since all traders know their location, pivot levels can influence the market participants' psychological reactions.

Therefore, they affect price movements.

The pivot is calculated from the previous bar or candle and can be measured over different time periods, sometimes even from the previous week or month. But, whatever the graph interval time they use while trading, traders consider the daily pivot most and it is indeed the most effective.

Taking the bar representing the previous day, the formula adds the high + low + close prices and divides the total by 3. Once the pivot level is known, the other points are calculated, to get the other supports and resistances, using the following method.

Support = 1 (Pivot X 2) - H

Support 2 = Pivot - (H - L)

Resistance 1 = (Pivot X 2) - L

Resistance 2 = Pivot + (H - L)

If the value remains above the pivot until mid-day, the trend will frequently keep rising for the rest of the day and if the first part of the session sees the value below its level, the rest of day will be down.

In an uptrend, a decline in price down to the pivot is to be purchased and in a downtrend, a return to the pivot is sold.

These levels are used to enter stops, facilitating risk management, and are more frequently used in liquid markets, such as indices.

To trade with the least possible complication, an entry position has to be in the direction of the trend, at a price level where several indications are accumulated, including the pivot, the regression back to touch the MA20, small candles of consolidation visible at the same price level and a decreased volume on the previous retracement. Thereupon, the stop is entered at a strategic level of support or resistance, to protect the trade.

The more reasons are gathered at the same price, the more the entry is likely to benefit.

When the trend is not too obvious, it is easy enough to change the time interval of the graph (time-frame) to get a clearer picture. Up, down or nonexistent has a major impact on the trader decision-making process.

The key is to recognize early a trend change and put trailing stops (exit orders, which advance with the price and are executed if the value returns by a set number of points). This allows the trader to accumulate profits until the stop is hit.

Over-elaborate technical analysis is not recommended, as it encumbers the graphs. The acquisition of a certain ease of use of the various simple tools is needed before using more complicated instruments. Moreover, even the greatest traders return to basic tools, when they have suffered heavy losses.

Once the trend is established, the lines of support and resistance are drawn and the price momentum is compared to the momentum indicators, to ensure that their orientation is in agreement. Recognizing the violation of a trend is often rewarded with profits, and avoids entering a trend-following trade when the direction appears in denial.

Usually, indicators are calculated based on the price of the instrument, giving a buy signal when their graph reaches an undervalued zone and a sell signal in its overvalued area.

For example the MACD, invented by Gerald Appel, is measured by the difference between two exponential moving averages (EMA), the most frequently used being those of 26 and 12 bars or candles. This variation (called the MACD) results in a line hovering below or above the zero line. Thereupon, a third exponential moving average of 9 bars, called the signal line, is added.

Thus, the crossing of the difference of the first two (26EMA and 12EMA) with the third (9EMA) gives a clue to purchase when the signal line crosses the MACD upward, while it is far away from the zero line, in the undervalued zone.

Opposite, a sell warning is given when the signal line crosses the MACD down, when that is in an overvalued area, above the zero level.

The exponential moving averages give more weight in the calculation to the most recent movements relative to the older, and as such, the MACD is more sensitive to recent changes in price.

However, the earlier the signal, the likelier it is to give a wrong indication. The disadvantage of the MACD, like any other indicator conventionally used, is that its reversal signals often lag behind the price.

FIG - MACD

As for the Relative Strength Index or RSI, it was developed in 1978 by Welles Wilder to measure the speed fluctuation of the value and compare the magnitude of a recent gain with the scale of a recent loss. This indicator represents the internal force of an instrument's move.

Using only a single parameter, usually 14 bars or candles, it indicates the intrinsic strength of a security by identifying its change of momentum. It is therefore an oscillator that measures the velocity of its direction.

If the price moves quickly on the rise, at some point it becomes overbought and therefore, the reversal is more likely. The curve of the indicator is proportional to the scope of the advance (or decline) and the information gives a score between 0 and 100. When the RSI reaches below 30, it generates a buy signal and when it goes above 70, it is a sell.

Two lines are drawn automatically to determine the levels of 30 and 70, in order to locate them more easily.

Another indicator, the "Stochastic Oscillator" shows the price momentum more intensely. Combined with other tools, it is very useful for giving a signal going against the trend to announce its end.

More effective than the MACD or the RSI to analyze trades anticipating a turnaround, the "Slow Stochastics" signals a shift lower if the intersection of its lines are above 80% of the value scale, and anticipates a move higher if they cross below the 20% level.

In an uptrending chart, when a trend line joining the highs of the stochastic indicator, the MACD or the RSI is heading in the opposite direction of the line joining the highs of the price graph, it is often a trend change alert and it is advisable not to trust the price still going upward.

The agreement (convergence) or the disagreement (divergence) of their tilt is the most useful property of any indicator, although it is necessary to confirm the facts with other tools.

The price continues higher while the stochastics are divergents and show a lower top than the previous one.

FIG - Stochastics

To check the hint of a reversal, confirmation can be obtained by adding the Williams Percent R, which estimates the price range on a number of bars, or the CCI, which can also determine an overvaluation or an undervaluation.

Another tool, from the studies of Leonard P. Ayers in the 1920s, is particularly useful for analyzing the overall "health" surrounding a price. Represented as a line, the "Advance-Decline" (ADD) allows speculators to measure a stock market's number of shares going upward or downward. A divergence is noted when the market is moving in one direction while this index is in the opposite direction.[5]

However, viewed in a traditional way, each of these indicators analyzes historical data and therefore, the previous prices. This means that their signal is often late, compared to the price, although if the trader considers the indicators convergence or divergence in relation to the price graph, the signal will be ahead and it will allow more profitable decisions.

Looking at several of these indicators, if they all show a convergence in line with the price chart, it confirms the established trend and the trader can enter a position going with the flow while being more confident of the momentum continuation. When a discrepancy is visible, a trade idea in the apparent direction of the price is dismissed, since warning is given that it is weakening. A combination of indicators is therefore regarded as a compass that confirms or refutes the current direction.

When, in a mutual agreement they report a divergence, an impending change of trend is considered and this deviation is significant as it is often far in advance of the price. This condition can also be used to bet against the market's visible trend.

Another indicator considers the speculators' mood. It is advisable to sell when they are euphoric, and buy when they are lamenting.

The Put / Call ratio estimates the volume of put options and compares it to the volume of Calls. The Put options are used to hedge against market weakness or to bet on its decline, and the Calls options are to leverage a bet on its strength or to anticipate its ascent.

---

5   Such a negative divergence was also observed at the end of the 1920-1929 bull market, during 1972 and the top of the market Nifty Fifty, towards the end of the dot-com bubble in the U.S. from 1999 to 2000, when the indices continued to rally while the AD Line diverged down from the beginning of 1999, and also from March 2008, before the collapse of the market until the end of 2008.

In general, this indicator is used to assess the perception of the market. An excessively bearish sentiment is seen when the Put / Call ratio is greater than 1, and the volume of bear bets exceeds the volume of the bulls. The opposite applies and the view of the environment is overly optimistic when the Put / Call ratio is much less than 1, the volume of speculative purchases exceeds that of sales. The Chartist can apply moving averages and other indicators to their graphical representation, to look at the data for signals for the Put / Call Ratio to rise or fall.

Its formula is simply the volume of Put options divided by the volume of Calls. As with the majority of opinion indicators, the quotient Put / Call is used as a contrary sign that allows the trader to evaluate the extreme levels, whether bullish or bearish.

When sentiment shows too optimistic an interpretation traders look for a downward market turn and, once the mood turns excessively pessimistic, they see it as a bullish forecast.

Indeed, the Put / Call Ratio considers the "mood swings" of positive or negative emotions and gives signals to buy if the euphoria makes the stock market overvalued or to sell when fear takes it to being undervalued.

This signal allows traders to position themselves in advance and anticipate the turn of events. Often, buying when panic is dominant will greatly reward speculators and this indicator is one of the tools to do so.

In general, options on indices are associated with professional traders and share options are associated with amateurs, which is why the quotient of options on indices is most influential. As such, the statistics from the Chicago Board Options Exchange (CBOE) are the most widely followed.

STOPS & TARGETS

*Affairs are easier of entrance than of exit; and it is
but common prudence to see our way out before we venture in.*

—*Aesop*

In the preparation of a plan, it is as necessary to seek reasons not
to trade, as justification confirming the potential of an entry. It is
a matter of capital preservation, to ensure that the trade really has
merit by piling up profit probabilities.

Stops are an integral part of the operation. They have to be
marked on the order book, or taken mentally if quantities are very
large, since "showing one's hand" is not recommended.

These orders are placed at a strategic level, to exit a trade
automatically as soon as the price is hit, "at the market". It is also
possible to specify the desired minimum price once the stop is
elected but in that case, the exit cannot be guaranteed.

One hazard of a long position kept several days is that its price
can open with a gap way down, for example 10 points lower, while
the stop has been placed at only two points below the previous day's
close.

Any unpleasant surprises, such as unexpected publication of
negative numbers or the announcement of a serious and unforeseen
event, can deter buyers until prices sell off to a level reflecting the
disappointment. Of course, the risk of a price gap is more common
in markets that close in the evening, like shares of stocks.

At the opening, the sell stop order is executed after the first opening "print" and the amount received is not minus two points, but rather ten. Thus, the risk calculation of the stop was wrong and replaced by a far larger deficit. In general, this is why rookie traders avoid taking a position just before the results of a company's earnings or when announcements regarding the economy are scheduled, to avoid a nasty shock.

This annoying price differential problem can also happen if the position is short. Following a "takeover" at a much higher price, the value can jump much higher, leaving a gap, and lose just as much, even if the stop level was tight.

Notwithstanding the possibility of unpleasant gaps, the stops are to be placed below support for purchases and above resistance for short sales. As the position earns, the stop can be changed to a new strategic level, as soon as the price indicates a safer place, locking in some of the profitable move.

Some traders also use trailing stops which advance with a predetermined price distance, to keep profits running until the end of the profitable move, without exiting too soon. Upon an entry at $20, a $.50 cents trailing stop would be at $19.50 and, as the price moves to $20.125 it is automatically changed to $19.625,[6] and so on.

If the number of transactions is intensive and orders sizes are less than ten thousand shares on a highly liquid market, it is possible to put the stops on the order book, and place two trades simultaneously, one at the stop-loss and the other at the target price, with an OCO order (One Cancels the Other). With this particular setup, once the target price is reached the stop is unnecessary and is automatically canceled or, if the stop is hit before the target, the latter is deleted.

Whatever the strategy and particularly for day trading, a profit target is always part of the trading plan.

---

6 At the time, the minimum price interval was one-eighth of a dollar, and therefore a value of $0.125, but today stocks trade at every cent.

Thus, among the many choices to set the price level at which the trader takes profits, the easiest way is also the most widely used by traders. First, it is necessary to calculate the risk, which is where the stop is strategically placed. Once defined, it is then quite easy to put a first exit for half the size at a price level for a gain equal to the risk (distanced from the entry for the same amount of money) and guaranteeing a safe trade, since that brings it to "break even". The second exit for the other half is placed for a net profit at least at twice the initial benefit.

Therefore, the risks are eliminated and the trade can be exploited longer.

As always, the easiest way is best.

ERRORS

Early in the career, it is normal for a beginner to make several missteps, but the number of errors progressively decreases and thus, the errors should become rare after several months of experience.

A study shows that a greater total of transactions made reduces the error rate:

TRADES (Quantity)	50	100	200	300	500
ERRORS (%)	14%	10%	7%	6%	4%

Over time, trading becomes innate and thus, fewer blunders are recorded.

But experience is acquired with real trades, the lessons learned becoming anchored in the trader's memory. Moreover, by keeping a journal reporting each operation in the late afternoon, before preparing the work plan for the next day, it is possible to acquire the practice much quicker, as each decision is taken into account.

Some of the small errors are:

✓ Entering a BUY instead of SELL: Pay Attention!

✓ Buying the wrong instrument, with a similar name or a similar symbol: Make sure name and symbol are checked!

✓ Placing a purchase limit to 13.0 when the price posted is 13.30, only to write 133.0, resulting in a price execution "at the market" for 13.40. Indeed, it is unpleasant. Take your time when entering orders and do not rush or panic.

These are small errors, but the big mistakes are unforgivable, as they often result in curtailing the length of the trader's career or even terminating it:

✓ Adding to a losing position to reduce the average cost (but with a larger quantity). "Never! Never average down." One of the trading laws is never to do that under any circumstances. A losing position has to be eliminated, not increased.

✓ Trading in a market without volume and liquidity. That is dangerous and can be dramatic![7]

✓ Not limiting losses. The study of the position size as well as the level at which the trade lost its merits are very important. Not having a stop will lead straight to disaster. Losses are part of the job, but a losing position has to be immediately eliminated.

✓ Staying "married" to a position, being paralyzed and seeing losses piling up. The key is to exit quickly.

Panicking results in a bad situation getting worse. A trader can lose his ability for reflection, analysis and decision making. The best way to avoid this risk is through proper preparation, market research and verification, as well as good knowledge and self-control. The trading plan, the stops and a good strategy do not invite fear.

---

7   In 1998, the hedge fund LTCM (Long Term Capital Management), led by Nobel Economic Sciences prizewinners, went bankrupt for investing in a market lacking liquidity. Without buyers to get rid of their very large positions, they suffered huge losses. They were leveraged and lost billions. Their failure could have resulted in a systemic crisis risking to implode the international financial system, but thanks to a rescue organized by the Fed, the danger was narrowly avoided.

✓ Over-trading (Taking too many positions). It is an indication of a lack of self-confidence and also a lack of preparation. This shows that the market direction is questionable and that the trader is not sure of anything.

✓ Greed: If the trader has come out of a winning trade, (being disciplined and following his plan), but sees the price continue its move without him, he becomes upset and enters a new trade without preparation, this mistake can cost him his previous earnings, and turn his profits into losses.

✓ Revenge: The trader has lost, but refuses to accept that he was wrong. He enters into another position because he is absolutely sure he is right, and , of course, he loses some more.

✓ Boredom: The trader is waiting, and still nothing happens, while he is thinking he has to trade to make money. However, entering a position without a plan and without thinking ahead is a mistake. Not trading is also not losing.

✓ Not having slept, being in a bad mood or upset can be detrimental to a trader's performance. Be sure to be in shape; it avoids problems.

✓ Wanting to recoup losses up, no matter what ... It only leads to more losses. After a series of bad trades and a significant capital reduction, the trader has to stop and take a break for a few days. Trying to be stronger than the market, or worse, trading with a bruised ego, is the best way to add to the difficulties.

✓ Losing perspective is also a big mistake. A trader should always keep in mind the "BIG PICTURE" (an overview of the market) in order to remain objective, while using an action plan designed to earn step by step, allowing him never to stray too far from the right road.

Losses & Mental Struggle

Success consists of going from failure to failure without loss of enthusiasm.

—Winston Churchill

Generally, if the preparation has not already covered all eventualities before emotions can surface, a losing trade can be crippling.

When a trader loses sleep because of a position, it is unhealthy. If he bites his nails and becomes worried sick, he shows clear symptoms of the consequences he now expects.

These signs disappear by exiting the trade.

Whatever the cause of anxiety, it is connected in one way or another to a lack of preparation, non-compliance with the strategy or risks taken which are clearly too great relative to the size of the portfolio.

In all cases, risk management rules have been ignored.

After suffering several losses, the reactions are often the same. As depression settles, some traders reduce their exposure with stops placed so near their entry that they deprive themselves of any opportunity for profit since no ease is left to the price movements, the stops being executed at the smallest market oscillation.

Others, when their account is largely down, cut a winning position too early in order to record a profit, however small. Evidently, being depressed by past mistakes adds new errors to the previous ones.

The reason for the embarrassment and the refusal to admit defeat comes from childhood. Very early, we are taught that losing is shameful. Aborting is dishonorable.

On the contrary, winning is widely praised and positive.

With this notion, embedded deep within ourselves, basic instinctive reactions are to deny a loss in the hope that everything will work out, or to presume that with more effort and intention to fight harder, we can eventually avoid this disgrace.

How to capitulate and accept losing?

To do this, a trader has to change his perspective to avoid rebellion taking over his thoughts. Because of pride, it is terribly difficult to accept quickly having been wrong and yet this simple admission is a vital reaction in trading. To let gains accumulate, previous errors must not be repeated, and losses have to be accepted. It is a deep psychological struggle, as each loss brings back fears settled into the subconscious, and emotions return to the memory at the slightest problem.

It is shown that, under stress, an adult's ability to think is reduced dramatically, his faculties reduced, although temporarily, to that of a toddler.

According to a medical book on emotions, an alarm system triggers in the head and causes this regression. It is an almond-shaped tissue found in the primitive part of the brain, which takes over during the struggle for survival.

Its name is the amygdala and it triggers panic, fight or paralysis of thought (Dr. Ledoux: *Cognitive-Emotional Interactions in the Brain*).

When the trader cannot stand the normal hazards of the job, he has to stop his activity for some time, to put his ideas back in place. This is a necessary safeguard, since a bad decision made under stress is enough to erase several days or even weeks of benefits.

THE ELLIOTT WAVE PRINCIPLE

You must live in the present, launch yourself
on every wave, find your eternity in each moment.

—*Henry David Thoreau*

It is quite understandable that market behavior depends on mass psychology. Feelings and emotional reactions move prices according to the mood and the perception of information. Such movements can be unexpected if the context in which the news is announced is ignored.

This is exactly the Elliott Wave theory, as are the Fibonacci retracements.[8]

The "Elliott Wave Principle" is the discovery of Ralph Nelson Elliott, who described the emotions of crowds, with thrusts and setbacks, forming recognizable patterns. Good market timing depends on the study of human behavior and psychology. The ever-changing path of stock prices reveals a structure reflecting a basic harmony, which is also found in nature. In a broad sense, the Elliott Wave theory proposes that the same law that shapes living creatures and galaxies, also influences the emotions and activities of men en masse.

Price movements are repetitive (fractals) and found in minor waves using hourly plots as well as in great annual wave cycles. At any time, the market can be identified as being at a certain level of waves, located itself in a degree of a broader pattern. Because the

---

8 Fibonacci retracements are covered at length in the chapter entitled "Fibonacci & Elliott" in Part One of this book.

wandering model is the basic form of market progression, all other models are divisions.

There are two modes of development: the impulse or motive and the retracement or corrective.

A complete cycle consists of eight waves, made of two distinct phases. The motive phase (also called a "five") is the major direction. The sub-waves are designated by numbers (1-2-3-4-5), and the correction phase (called a "three") reveals the reverse reaction, whose waves are designated by letters (ABC). Most of the motive waves are driving pulses, and their extensions are lengthened pulses with exaggerated subdivisions.

Inside the motive phase, wave 2 never retraces more than wave 1, wave 4 never comes back further than the start of wave 3, and wave 3 always goes further than wave 1. The objective of a motive wave is to advance, and therefore this rule helps ensure the correct interpretation.

In terms of price, wave 3 is often the longest, and is never the shortest among the three main waves (1, 3 and 5) of a motive pattern. As long as wave 3 represents a greater length percentage than the wave 1 and 5 movements, this rule is satisfied. In addition, waves of impulse (1, 3 and 5, as well as A and C) are themselves divided into mini motor phases (1-2-3-4-5), especially the third, while corrective phases (2-4, and B) are divided into 3 mini phases (a-b-c).

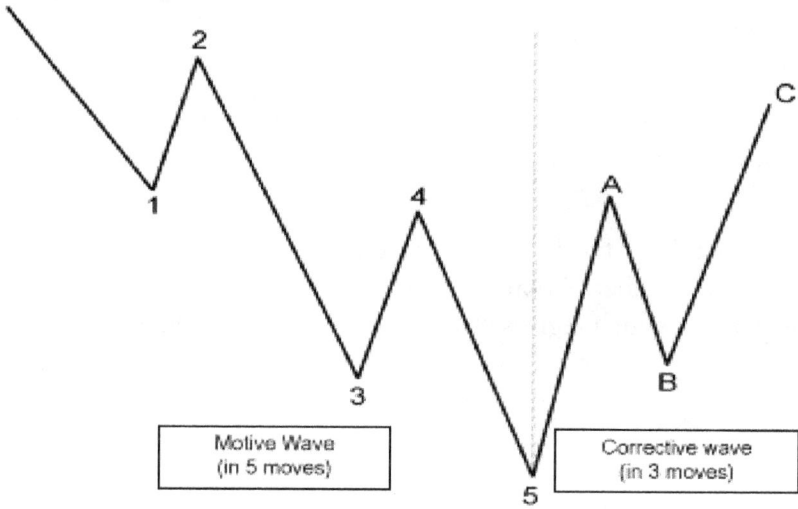

FIG - Elliott Wave Theory

The term "truncated" is used to describe a situation in which the fifth wave does not move beyond the end of the third. A truncated wave can usually be verified by noting that the wave presumed to be the fifth wave contains the five subdivisions necessary, and is produced after a long and powerful wave 3.

If the extension of the fifth wave ends in a truncated triangle or diagonally, this infers a dramatic reversal is coming. If two of these occur in varying degrees, the movement in the opposite direction will be all the more violent.

The volume allows verification of the waves count and projection of their extensions, by decreasing in correction phases. A weak point in volume often coincides with a turning point in the market. Thus, the fifth wave has less volume than the previous four.

The Elliott Wave principle clearly appears in the financial charts because the stock market is the best reflector of crowd psychology in the world. It is the manifestation of the psychological and social conditions of man, which determine the fluctuation of his business production and thus, engender phases of progress and regression.

The Wave principle allows the observation that the development of humanity does not happen in a straight line and at random, but rather that it is advancing at a rate of "three steps forward, two steps back" as in nature.

The market depicts a mass behavior that can be studied and defined, using a simple mathematical formula: the golden ratio 1.618.

The study of the Elliott theory ensures that, coincidence or not, the actual number of points in the motive waves are 1.618 as part of the pattern, which regress by a 0.618 ratio, as in the Fibonacci series.

STRATEGIES

The real heart of strategy is the strategist.

—*Max McKeown*

Naturally, any preparation uses strategies.

Before the opening, the potential to trade in a security begins with the possibility of applying a method that determines the conditions under which the probability of success is the best possible.

The strategy rules stipulate the conditions that have to be present to expect best results and, once the order is placed, they indicate the location of the stop, which has to be placed at a level where the transaction has lost its merit. Then, often based on the risk bounded by the stop, the profit target is decided.

The simplest formulas are often the most successful. Besides, it is often when a beginner thinks he understands the system that he begins complicating things, which can result in less profitable operations.

Obviously, it is advisable to use the KISS principle (Keep It Simple, Stupid) and to stick to using only the most effective configurations. The goal is not to be a hero, but to follow a program perfectly, which allows the trader to earn money with the least possible risk.

There is no need to adopt a multitude of different strategies; just a few are sufficient to make money quite regularly, and they become innate.

The trend-following strategy first requires a strong upward trend, with the moving averages situation showing the MA10 above the

MA20, which is itself above the MA50, while the 20 and 50 periods are parallel and trending up along the price.

Before anything else, it is necessary to confirm the strength of the trend with the analysis of a graph of higher time interval. The same behavior of higher highs and higher lows strengthen the assumption of direction continuation.

So, once assured that the general inclination is bullish, the idea to open a trade is considered if the price has spiked up to distance itself from the MA20. The trader has to wait for a retracement, which brings the price back down, with decreased volume, to touch the MA20. The signal to enter is given by a very small positive candle, indicating that the price has the potential to rise again, ending its pull back.

The small indecision candle (trigger) can also be a Dragon Fly, a Doji or another, looking like a pinhead and called a Hammer, these patterns being bullish and auguring a higher price. The fact is, that a small or particularly optimistic candle means that the battle between buyers and sellers is difficult but the fight is won by the buyers.

After making sure that several indicators are convergent, with the uptrend price also showing higher highs (agreeing), that they are not in an overvaluation area and they do not have their lines crossed there (which would be negative and a "no go"), the trade has merit. Also, if a level of support and a pivot point are found nearby, preventing the price from going lower and therefore protecting the position, these add weight to the arguments of trading long (buy).

In addition, if the price regression going back down to touch the MA20 is half or two-thirds of the strong initial advance (most retrace in this way, at the Box Fibonacci), this move corresponds to three steps forward and two steps back, simply representing the growth of nature. This condition adds another reason to the idea of purchase, indicating the resumption of the uptrend.

The potential entry can be placed in advance by a buy order if the price goes again above the positive trigger candle, proving it is not a ""once and done" bullish bar.

The stop is located just below this same trigger bar since if the price goes lower, it would prove that it is not the end of the retracement. Another place for a stop, although it involves more risk, is to place it just below the last low, since if the price fell below that low, it would deny the uptrend hypothesis.

FIG - Trend flow Strategy

In a downtrend, it is simply the opposite, with a visible small negative candle triggering the signal, an inverted hammer or a Doji, indicating uncertainty among sellers and buyers at the touch of the MA20, and following a retracement with a smaller volume, while the moving averages are heading down and show a parallel track with the price. Pivot points can also be considered to add arguments to the idea of transaction. As always, if the bounce back of part of the descent in price accounts for half or two-thirds of it, ending with a negative trigger candle, it indicates the short entry, which anticipates the continuation to the downside.

Another strategy is also to follow a well-established trend, when the position of the price is close to its 20-period moving average.

In all trades anticipating a trend continuation, it is necessary to consider a longer interval graph, confirming the price direction, and it is imperative that the indicators be converging with the price, showing higher highs in an uptrend and lower lows in a downtrend.

As well as the previous strategy, the combination of other indicators meeting at the same level authenticate the entry and give more weight to the probabilities of a profitable transaction.

In that second strategy, the basic principle is that the price is faced with a strong support (in a bearish chart) or a strong resistance (in a bullish chart) and is not able to go through that flat level, despite trying several times. If the candles are becoming smaller and more crowded while getting closer to the line, without being able to pass the apparently unbreakable wall, the trade is considered.

In an uptrend, if the indicators also show the higher high or at least follow the price indicating that they would go higher at the same time as the price, the arrival of a breakout through the resistance line will be with such momentum that the chances of winning are major. The order can be placed in advance, just above the resistance line. The breakout effect will be similar to the steam of a pressure cooker, with a powerful jet due to the energy built up.

If, and only if, the price breaks through the solid line of resistance, the trade is entered on this break, with a stop below the latest low of the uptrend in price, since beyond this level, it would cancel the assumption of an uptrend and thus, would make the transaction invalid.

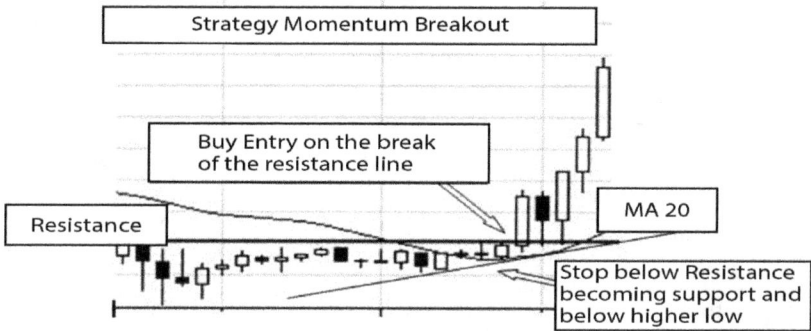

FIG - Strategy Momentum Breakout

For a downward trend it is the opposite, passing through an important support which has been touched many times in vain, is the entry of a sale.

And then, another tactic is useful, this time to speculate against the established trend. Although this strategy presents more risks, the results are sometimes very beneficial.

This third configuration analyzes the potential reversal of a very low price, seen at a market floor and signaled by a candle Dragon Fly, a Doji or a Hammer as trigger. A more significant indication is that the price, after making a new low, goes over the top of the previous bar and, better yet, trades higher than the last five.

If the indicators are divergent (the price still makes lower lows while several indicators show higher lows), the idea of a reversal is considered.

For additional argument, if the "Slow Stochastics" have crossed upward in their undervalued area below 20% and the Bollinger Bands are exceeded down, but the trigger bar close is inside, the probabilities of a price move up are increased.

The stop is placed immediately below the trigger candle (Doji, Hammer or any other positive figure) as a new low annuls the assumption of an ending bear market.

FIG - Strategy Trend Reversal

In the opposite direction, this configuration is for a strong bull market, where a warning candle, like a Doji, a Gravestone or an inverted hammer, indicates the possibility of a reversal down. While the price has continued to make higher highs, indicators already show lower highs and moreover, they have crossed in their area of overvaluation.

Whatever the strategy chosen, the trader has to seek all possible additional reasons that will increase the potential to profit. The more tools are accumulated to give a signal at the same level, the more a trade has potential for success.

Many other strategies exist, but using only a few is enough to make money. The only requirements are not to risk more than 2% on each trade, to comply with the rules and to be disciplined. The secret of success is found in good risk management, while avoiding the exposure of too much capital to chance. It is important to recognize that a position taken in the same direction as the stock index is more likely to succeed, and that keeping a balance between purchases and sales positions is to be recommended, while tilting the equilibrium to an increase of short positions in a bear market and an increase to long ones, in a rising market.

CHECKLIST TREND-FOLLOWING STRATEGY

(Do the opposite for downtrend.)

Conditions:

The general market is confirmed to be in an uptrend and is also going up. Its behavior is proven by higher highs and higher lows (it is safer to trade in the same direction as the stock market).

The larger time interval graph has confirmed the direction of the trend.

The Moving Averages 10-20 and 50 periods are parallel to the price and are heading in the direction of the trend.

The price has gone way up fast, getting away from its MA20, but comes back down slowly to touch it again, with low volume on the decline.

The retracement back is 50% to 61.8% of the advance, measured from bottom to top, if the market is volatile. If the market is quiet, it may only be between 38.2% and 50%.

The decline is stopped at a pivot point.

Indicators are converging (in the same direction) with the price, showing higher highs (a divergence would cancel the possibility of transaction).

The indicators are not in a zone of overvaluation and do not cross.

Bar or candle touching the MA20 has the form of a Doji, a Hammer or is very small and positive.

There are no visible resistance levels between the position entry and the intended target. If a support level protects the location of the stop, this is an advantage.

Entry: When the price trades higher than the top of the trigger candle near the MA20 (signaling the resumption of the rise)

Stop 1: On the price trading lower than the bottom of the

trigger candle (indicating that it is not the end of the decline, which is, therefore, not completed).

Stop 2: Just below the last low of the uptrend chart, since its break indicates a change in trend, denying the hypothesis of an uptrend.

Exit 1: Get out of half the position at a realized gain equal to the level representing the loss (risk) of Stop 1.

Exit 2: Let profits run and move the stop once a new strategic level of protection is found.

CHECKLIST - TREND REVERSAL STRATEGY

(Do the reverse at the end of a downtrend)

Conditions:

The general market is already bearish (it is safer to trade in the same direction as the stock market).

The chart considered shows an overheated price.

The confirmation chart of a much higher time interval (for 15mn, consider the daily graph) shows the instrument to be in a bear market and the overheated price is but a retracement in an overall down graph.

The price made a new high, but turned around to close on its low.

Close is not only at the bar low but lower in price than the previous bar. (Lower than the last 5 bars would be better!)

Extreme overvaluation and price divergence with several indicators. While a line connecting the tops of the price is going up, a line joining the highs of the RSI and the Stochastics (or MACD), shows lower highs.

Volume decreased over the last 5 bars upward.

Volume of the trigger down bar is approaching twice the volume of the last 10 bars.

CCI has crossed down a number of bars earlier in its overvalued zone, and is heading down.

Stochastics are crossing down above their 80%.

The price has risen above the Bollinger Bands but closed inside them.

Entry: If the price trades below the bottom of the reversal candle (indicating the continuation of the decline).

Stop 1: At the level where the price trades back above the trigger reversal candle (showing renewed rise).

Stop 2: 2% above the top of the reversal candle (sometimes a strong upward trend implies a refusal to capitulate and the price can break the previous high, before a much more drastic fall).

Exit 1: Get out of half the position at a realized gain equal to the level representing the loss (risk) of Stop 1.

Exit 2: Let profits run and move the stop once a new strategic level of protection is found.

TURTLE TRADING

However beautiful the strategy, don't forget to look at the results.

—*Winston Churchill*

There is another trading strategy worth mentioning.

By pure chance, early in my career I discovered a trading system called "Turtles". It was a mysterious method, revealed under the promise of secrecy after the Crash of 1987, once the experiment had ended.

The system had been created a few years earlier by a former Mid-American Exchange trader, who became a millionaire at twenty-five years old, accumulating enough profit to buy a full membership on the Chicago Board of Trade. He made a bet with his friend that he could teach the novice how to trade, like the turtles could be raised in Singapore, from where he had just returned.

This experiment was designed to discover whether traders were born with what it takes to succeed, or if it was the experience that made them win. Eighty people were initially recruited, but this group was reduced to only thirteen individuals. They were quite ordinary people, without special qualities, trained to become traders in a fortnight, with a trend-following strategy.

Next, each of them was allowed to trade on the markets for a maximum of twelve contracts in total and then, based on the performance they had obtained after a month's trial, an amount ranging from five hundred thousand to two million dollars was given to each, so that they could trade by applying this method.

It allowed the youngest of them to earn more than thirty million dollars in four years.

Each system, and this one in particular, pays strict attention to the size of the position. The basis of a good trader is to have risk control. "Turtles trading" was no exception and the operators had to "normalize volatility" which was a fancy way of reducing the position if an instrument was more volatile, meaning that each trade would carry a similar risk to the capital.

'N' is the name given to an exponential moving average of 20 days of the ATR (Average True Range). Its formula is:

(19 x PDN (the previous day N) added to the True Range (or motion of the day) divided by 20.

Since the formula for 'N' asks for the previous day N, it means starting with 20 days and only then is the formula 19xN + TR/20. The ATR is calculated by finding the greater value among the following three results:

- The distance between the top and bottom of the day,

- The distance between the closing of the day and the high of the day, and

- The distance between the closing of the day and the low of the day, and including all gaps of any price.

Once the ATR 20 is noted, it is necessary to understand the "Adjusting Dollar volatility" which is simply (dollars per point x N). This is done in order to calculate the size of a so-called "unit". Each "unit" takes into account 1% stake of the operator's capital. In other words, one unit is equivalent to:

1% of the account / Dollar volatility.

For example, according to the position, if an instrument moves by $100 per point and the account size is ten thousand dollars, then N = 1/10th, one unit being 1% of the account divided by (N x Dollars per point).

That to say (1% x $10,000) / (0.1 X $100), which is $10.

The Turtles could theoretically start the year with one million dollars, but in the case of a 10% loss, the account was reduced by 20%. In other words, the trader saw his account become even smaller, which required him to take less risk, as if he had only eight hundred thousand dollars, and not the nine hundred thousand remaining, until the account returned to the original figure.

The trading method was based on two strategies, a trend breakout system of 20 days and another of 55 days.

To use the first system in a rising market, if the price breaks through the line connecting all the tops of the previous 20 days during the session (or if it opens above), it is a signal to enter one unit, which is purchased, to start position. The reverse is true for a downtrend, the break lower of the low of last 20 days, is a signal to sell one unit.

However, if the preceding signal has led to a successful transaction, the new signal is ignored in order to avoid too many "zigzag motions."

The second system gives a buy signal if the price has exceeded the high of last 55 days (or breaks below the lows of the last 55 days) and contrary to the policy of 20 days, these positions are always taken, regardless of the success or failure of the previous trade.

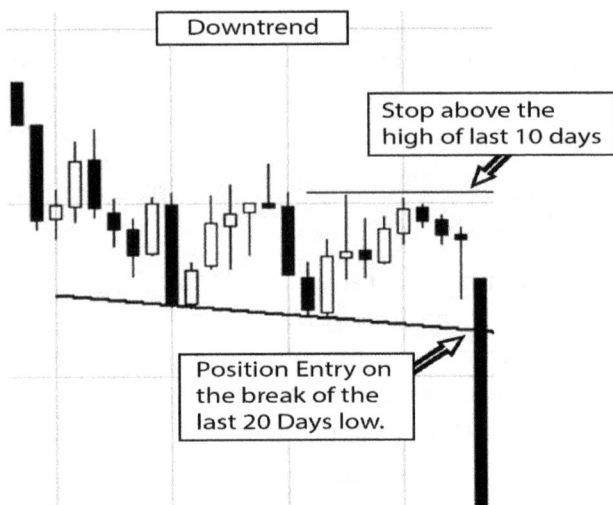

FIG - Turtles Strategy

Once in position, the Turtles added an additional unit every 1/2 'N' earnings up to the maximum number of units that they were allowed to accumulate (four in one instrument, six markets "highly correlated" such as crude oil in relation to Brent, ten units in the markets "weakly correlated", and a total of twelve units in one direction).

The main directive in all this is consistency. As the majority of transactions fail, it is essential to perform each perfectly, so as not to miss the few winners who gain, alone, huge profits and largely compensate for the losers.

Their stops and outputs: No trader was allowed to risk more than 2% of his capital - in other words, the Turtles used a mental stop, and could not risk more than 2 'N' from the position entry. However, for any unit added, whenever the price rose 1/2 N, the previous unit's stop would be raised up by 1/2 N and, as long as the position earned, units were added to the maximum allowed.

To exit the first system (20 Days breakout), if the bottom of the last 10 days (for purchase) has been broken, that means the trade should be closed. Similarly, if the top of the last 10 days is broken (for a short sale), the position is closed immediately. To exit the second system (55 days), the breaking of the last 20 days in the opposite direction gives the signal.

The Turtles were great traders, as they needed to have a strong discipline. This trading style called for an iron will, to be able to follow the rules perfectly, without trying to "bend" the mechanics of the formula.

Thus, the Turtles could only comply with them.

The most difficult was probably to be mentally equipped to deal with constant losses, even if losses were handsomely recovered by the winning trades.

For most people, it would be unbearable.

A great strength of character was imperative, but the results were spectacular.

My Formulas

My formulas for trend reversal include a long list of different ingredients and tools, fine-tuned during my thirty-six months of back-testing.

My system uses the Bollinger Bands, a trading tool created in the 1980s by John Bollinger, which are represented by two lines used as "Standard Deviations" around a 20 periods Moving Average, and are used to determine whether the prices are high or low in relation to their history. The method is derived from the observation that volatility is dynamic and not static.

In a moderate inclination, the Bollinger Bands are used as a channel with the establishment of a purchase if the price touches the bottom band and a sell if the price comes in contact with the top band, while following the established trend.

According to their creator, the price should stay contained within the bands in 88% of cases.

Resistance

MA 20

Bolligen Bands tightening and breakout

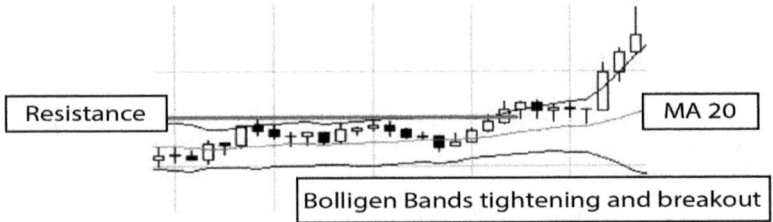

FIG - Bollinger Bands & Momentum Breakout

Their calculation is largely influenced by the close of each candle and when the bands tighten to get very close, a major move can be expected, causing a change sometimes brutal in price before they can gradually return to a more normal distance from the Moving Average between them.

Channel with Price
Support and Resistance

Bollinger Bands

Break of the inferior band and close inside
of them with small hesitation candles

Volume

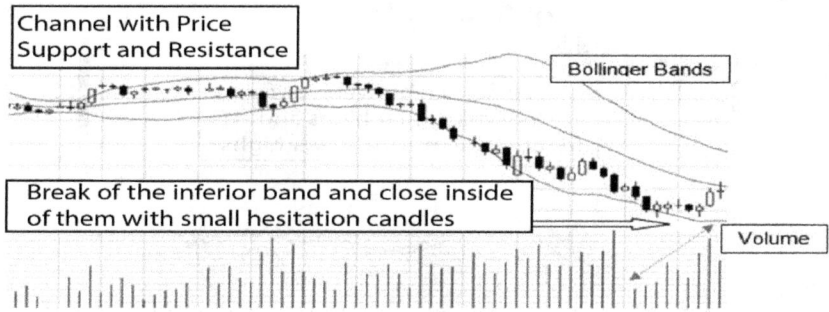

FIG - Bollinger Bands and Reversal

Another example of using the Bollinger Bands is when the trend is down for a long time and each bar has touched the bottom band. If the price falls below the lower band but comes back to close inside, it has potential to reverse. After a short consolidation where several small candles appear at the same level, a rise in price can be anticipated, particularly if the base has formed with a higher volume on positive candles. This purchase is made after a visible signal, the trigger candle having the shape of a Doji or a Hammer.

The stop is then placed just below the last price low.

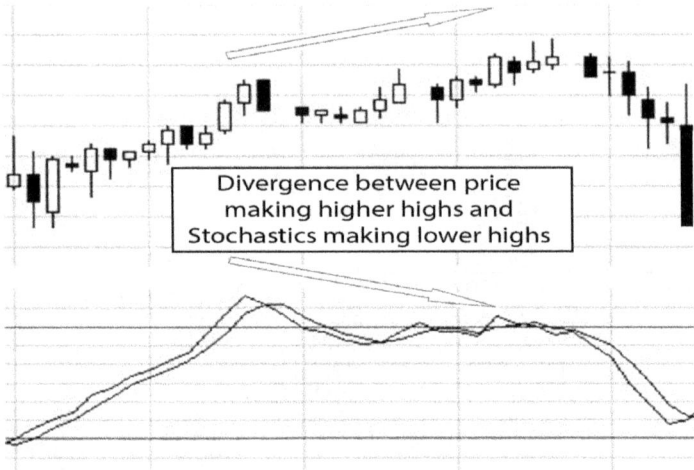

FIG - Divergence Stochastics

Among my best configurations tools are the Slow Stochastics. Dr. George Lane developed this momentum indicator in 1954, after his teachers began the research, and according to him, this indicator was to be used with cycle analysis, the Elliott Wave principle and the Fibonacci retracements.

Its formula is to take the closing price and to compare it to its price range, over a period of time. Apparently, the "Stochastic Oscillator" does not follow the price and does not follow the volume; it obeys the momentum speed of the price.

The sensitivity of the oscillator to market movements makes it essential, since its evolution will change direction before the price. As such, a bullish or bearish divergence can better signal a reversal of the value and therefore, announce a change in trend.

The theory behind this indicator is that in a bull market, prices generally close near their high, and in a bear market, the closing is near their lowest point.

A transaction signal is given when the moving average of three bars or candles (called %D) cross through the 14 bars (%K). If the %D crosses %K up, below 20% of the graph, it is a buy signal and when the crossing is down, above the 80% level, the signal is to sell.

When drawing a trend line on the Stochastics, if its tilt shows a divergence with the direction of the price graph, it is often an indication of a trend change, or at least a weakening of the visible direction.

Combined with other analyses the regular use of the Stochastics is very helpful, giving a signal that goes against the trend to announce its end.

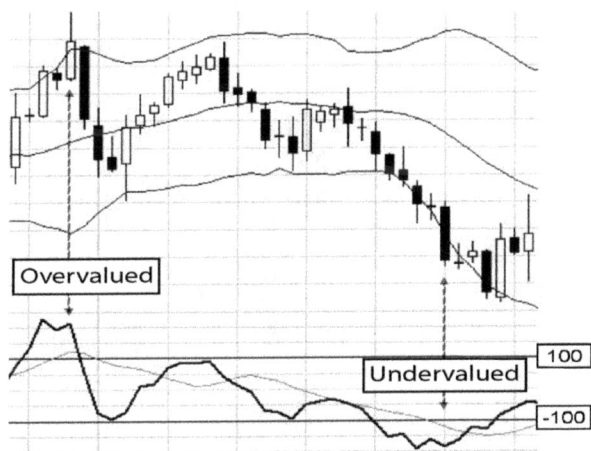

FIG - CCI

Another useful indicator, the CCI, was created by Donald Lambert in 1980.

It was originally designed for commodities, hence its name "Commodity Channel Index", but it has been adopted in all markets. It looks a little like the "Stochastic Oscillator", although is more volatile.

A high level CCI indicates an overvalued price and gives the incentive to sell. A very low CCI reports an undervalued price and purchase can be considered.

REMINISCENCES OF A WALL STREET TRADER

To filter the small changes and only keep the most relevant information, two levels are plotted on the graph, at 100 and -100. According to the inventor, most of the oscillations are realized inside these levels and they are not interesting.

Therefore, as the level varies between -100 and 100, there is no suggestion and the graph is supposed to be in a consolidation period. But above 100, a decline is anticipated and below -100, an increase is considered.

The combination of these indicators is at the heart of my formulas.

STATISTICS

Facts are stubborn, but statistics are more pliable.

—*Mark Twain*

Before being around traders, I thought one of the major conditions to be part of the trading profession was to be a great mathematician. I also anticipated that statistics would play a much more important role, only to find I was wrong on both counts.

The only expression from statistics mentioned from time to time, is the "standard deviation" which in general, is used to refer to long-term positions and not rapid trading.

In statistics, the rule of a normal distribution is that a value moving away from its average will only get to maximum distance of three units and that all measures remain in an area within 99.7% of it. Then, at a distance of two units away are 95% of the values and, finally at one, are 68.2% of them. Obviously, in the case where the distance was between 99.7% and 100%, it would be an event so rare in theory of probability that if it occurred, it would most likely take the form of serious and very unusual accident.

The improbability and the surprise would certainly cause a significant impact.[9]

In statistics and probability theory, the standard deviation shows how the variation or "dispersion" compares to the average or expected value.

---

9 In 2001, in his book *Fooled By Randomness* Nassim Taleb gave the name of "Black Swan" for such an eventuality. As rare and unpredictable as it is, this circumstance can bring value by a quite spectacular departure from the average.

A short distance from the mean indicates that the points referenced tend to be very close to equilibrium, whereas a large gap from it reveals that these are spread over a wide range of values. The standard deviation of a random variable set of elements or the probability distribution being the square root of its variance, it has the property to be expressed in the same units as the data, unlike the actual random variance.

Standard deviation is commonly used to measure confidence in statistical conclusions, the margin of error reported being typically about twice the standard deviation - the radius of a confidence interval of ninety five percent.

In finance, the standard deviation (SD) rate of return on an investment is a measure of the volatility of this investment and therefore this is an important indication to examine the risks of a portfolio.

But to evaluate short-term trading, it is not necessary to calculate the deviations from the mean. Good risk management and fierce discipline allows the trader to stay in the area of positive results. The danger is to try to earn a lot more by taking bold risks. Moreover, it is universally recognized that the best traders earn slowly, but surely.

This principle seems to be the key to success.

Thus, my only use of the standard deviation remains in technical analysis with the Bollinger Bands.

Another study in statistics and probabilities is to measure the correlation. Again, there is no absolutely necessary reason to apply it in day-trading; the only reciprocity sought is made by examining the behavior of stocks in relation to their sector or their benchmark, which is easily seen from looking at their quote.

As for a hedge fund's reporting, it is possible to obtain from the accountants the portfolio performance evaluations, whether at month-end, quarter-end or year-end.

These reports peel results and derive statistics from its history or in comparison to the general market, which frees the trader to be concerned about nothing else than making money.

FUNDAMENTAL ANALYSIS

In the last analysis, what we are communicates
far more eloquently than anything we say or do.

— *Stephen R. Covey*

Fundamental Analysis examines the business performance of an enterprise, the quality of its management, its profit potential and the probability of expansion as well as its derivatives, to determine if the current value (quote) is overvalued or undervalued. Comparing the latest quarterly results to the previous ones and estimating the general "health" of the sector in which the company belongs, the report is used to define the possibility of a rise in price of the investment considered.

The review also includes the economic and political situation of the moment, as well as the news that may affect the value of the business, good or bad. A good proficiency of the macro and microeconomics is required for effectively understanding the data and making the correct decisions. But often, this research faces surprises as some hidden facts are revealed much later, to dramatically affect the market. That is why it is really necessary to combine fundamental analysis with technical analysis, the latter being able to raise a red warning flag, while the data doesn't yet unveil anything.

Often, novice traders make the mistake of not considering a general view of the environment. Professionals take into account "The Big Picture", a more complete perspective, in order to anticipate the growth potential of a company.

As such, the sector to which the stock belongs is very important and, in many ways, the best investments come first from the selection among the industries, and then the choice of company. A "top-down" analysis is to start from the global point of view, beginning with the industry and next, to examine the specific details. After all, an average company in a winning sector is generally better off than a leading company in an industry in freefall.

Then, it is necessary to develop an understanding of the functioning of that enterprise, to check the relative strength of its balance sheet, the efficiency of its administration and the prospects of future earnings. In addition, it is essential to know its products, to evaluate their popularity, to study their costs relative to their sales and to see the profit margins they generate.

Internal factors are generally classified as Strengths and Weaknesses, while external factors are recorded as Opportunities and Threats (SWOT). For example, it is important to investigate whether the company has a good reputation for its patents, if it owns brands or superior craftsmanship, and if it has exclusive access to certain resources or to a preferential distribution network. This study can be extremely helpful when one wants to understand the competitive environment of an organization and ensure that it uses its strengths, to take advantage of its resources and its capabilities, to develop a competitive advantage over its competitors.

One should also take into account the threats. Dangers usually reside outside the company, like the opportunities. Alerts can come from a change in the consumers' taste, competitive services or the development of alternative products, as well as new government regulations or new trade barriers.

However, day trading is much less efficient if it relies on fundamentals. Short-term trading is most affected by hype, the news, or the media's market perception of the moment. In short, day-trading is reactive.

Some traders have developed fairly sophisticated models to take advantage of opportunities associated with events related to earnings announcements, to respond to analysts' "upgrades" and "downgrades" (positive or negative recommendations) and also, they have a method for the stock splits.

For example, a stock split 2 for 1 means that the price is halved, while the investor receives in exchange twice the number of shares he has owned. The method is to buy shares on the announcement of a stock split, and to sell short if it is a reverse-split, which is to have half the securities at a doubled price.

For acquisitions and reorganizations, traders buy in principle the company that is coveted and sell short the acquiring one, since the acquisition entails going into debt. As for IPOs, the interest depends on the sector and the growth potential.

These strategies are tested, clever and, although not infallible, they generate profits by correctly identifying the price movements that may occur later.

The key is to be well prepared to deal with any event and, most importantly, to fully understand news and data.

Fundamental analysis is the territory of analysts, working as support staff for the money-makers, the traders. While traders see the information as valuable, they have to add technical analysis to the results before deciding on a trade, as the performance is improved by good timing.

CYCLES ANALYSIS

Rule number one : most things will prove to be cyclical

*Rule number two : some of the greatest opportunities for
gain and loss come when other people forget rule number one.*

—Howard Marks (Oaktree)

While nature's cycles are visible and predictable, those of the
market are confusing, as small cycles interfere with the larger ones
and conceal their evidence. Despite this fact, some instruments
have repeated patterns, showing more or less regularly. For example,
agricultural commodities cycles are quite understandable because
their price depends on crops and seasons.

Cotton, soybeans and corn see their spot price reach its lowest
point of the year in the fall, during harvest. Therefore, their cost
influences the livestock (cattle, hogs), which reach a price floor at
the same time.

Then, wheat and oats generally have their minimum value
during the summer, which is the period of their harvest. Their costs
reflect the seasonal supply and demand and depend on the time of
production and need.

A trader knows that the price will not go lower than the season's
low (except for rare events) until an episodic high can be established,
several months later.

All fundamental results are insufficient because they are only
known after the fact. That's why it seems wise for traders to use the

study of cycles and technical analysis, to predict the likelihood of price movements and trend change, even before the numbers are announced.

For this study, it is first necessary to define the dominant cycles (annual) affecting the instrument's quote. Those findings are then combined with the analysis of shorter cycles (weeks and months).

Most markets have small cycles, ranging from 14 to 35 days and, by combining them the trader can detect an intermediate cycle of 6 to 20 weeks, from a low to another low of the chart, depending on the market studied.

Cycles diagrams are rarely symmetrical with each other, and different examples are to be noted:

- 9 years for wheat,

- 5½ years for corn and precious metals,

- 25 to 38 months for soybeans,

- 11 years for livestock, and

- 4 years for the business cycle.

But, more important is to consider the 60-year cycle governing equity markets and, therefore, the SP500, the index of reference for most.

Economy

There can be economy only where there is efficiency.

—*Benjamin Disraeli*

The health of a market is proven to be largely dependent on the health of its country's economy, so financiers analyze carefully any information regarding the latter.

The market value can really go up or down significantly after economic news.

One of the biggest reactions often occurs following an announcement from the Fed, the central bank of the United States. Even if interest rates remain unchanged, the wording of the comments published in the press is peeled, word for word, to try to guess what the committee may decide in the future.

Another important event is the report on the employment situation, and other reports on regional conditions have their own impact with the Beige Book, the Empire State index of New York and the one from the Philadelphia Fed, to which are added some more general evaluations, like the health of the ISM index (manufacturing production).

Traders take into account some guidelines that can raise an alarm or reassure them on the state of the economy.

For example, if the yield on short-term government bonds (duration 90 days) is higher than the rate of those that are long-term (duration 10 years) and this situation lasts for more than three months, it is a bad omen for the health of the state.

An inverted yield curve turns out to be a very unfortunate sign, ominous for the future.

Also, some economic markers are considered leaders, or ahead of others to predict what will happen later. These included factories' new orders and average hours worked, the unemployment, the SP500 value, consumers' expectations and the 10 years interest rate compared with that of monetary funds.

In addition, if these "leading indicators" (which outstrip the economic behavior of the country) are continuously downhill over a period of six months and the ratio of "coincident to lagging indicators" is heading down for two quarters, traders can be ready to change their positive view of the market, as these indications report that a recession is imminent.

This prediction is equally valid in the case of the GDP (Gross Domestic Product) being down over several quarters in a row, or if the country's unemployment increases by 1.5% or more over the year.

However, contrary to the assumptions made by some people, a country with a debt exceeding its GDP is not necessarily on the verge of bankruptcy.

These details have to be taken into account to manage any portfolio, even for day-trade negotiations since short-term trading benefits greatly from reactions caused by economic announcements.

PERFORMANCES EVALUATION

True genius resides in the capacity for evaluation of
uncertain, hazardous, and conflicting information.

—*Winston Churchill*

Hedge funds are interesting to investors because they are associated with the concept of "absolute returns". It is this feature that makes them so attractive, especially when markets are bearish. This approach differs from mutual funds, which are measured against their own benchmarks, their performance being compared to that of their sector.

As such, when mutual funds have negative results, their final outcome remains acceptable as long as they are marginally better than their benchmark.

A hedge fund on the other hand, has to provide absolute returns, regardless of conditions. The portfolio performance is assessed against a number of risk factors, and it is important for the manager to take each of them into account when making his decisions. In this respect, they can be compared to valuation models.

"VaR" (Value at Risk or risk of loss) is a predictive tool to prevent portfolio managers from exceeding the risk tolerance agreed upon in the charter. It represents a threshold value that the probability of a "mark-to-market" loss on a portfolio will exceed its value, over a period of time, assuming normal market conditions and no trading. VaR is a percentile of the predictive probability allocation for the size of a future loss, taking into account the distribution of investment fund profits and losses, the insurance required in order to be able to get a higher or equal return to the VaR, and the performance in the time period analyzed. This is done assuming a normal asset behavior, which is assumed to have remained similar, based on history.

The Capital Asset Pricing Model (CAPM) is used to evaluate prices in a market equilibrium and indicates that the expected return of a security or of a portfolio has to be equal to the rate of a risk-free security, plus a risk premium. The model is based on a specified return required by an investor. The rate of risk-free money is, in principle, represented by the rate of a government bond (usually a 10 year Treasury Bond), increased by a risk premium related only to the market risk of the asset. If this return cannot match or beat the specified expectation, the investment should not be undertaken.

CAPM introduces the concept of Alpha, which involves factors related to the performance of an investment or fund; it is an active, risk-adjusted measure of profit. Because alpha represents profit beyond compensation for the risk taken, alpha is commonly used to evaluate the performance of asset managers. Often the outcome of a benchmark is subtracted from the result, in order to show the relative performance.

Typically, the SP500 index is taken as the indicator of choice for the market as a whole, and a second measurement, Beta, measures the volatility representing the systematic risk of a security or a portfolio relative to the market.

Thus, beta is calculated using regression analysis; it is possible to think of beta as the tendency of the returns of a security to respond to market fluctuations. A beta value of 1 indicates that the stock price moves proportionally with the market. Since its volatility correlates to its benchmark, a stock with a beta of one is often a very large cap weighing considerably on the overall measurement and contributing to the index.

A beta of less than 1 means that the returns from the stock tend to react less, in percentage terms, than the market and a beta greater than 1 indicates that the stock price is more volatile than the market.

For example, if the beta of a share is 1.2, theoretically it is 20% more volatile than the SP500 index and if the latter goes down by 1%, then that stock can be expected to go down by 1.2%.

Many utilities have a beta less than 1 and, at the other end of the spectrum, the high-tech securities have a beta much greater than 1, which offers the possibility of a higher growth rate, but carries the risk of higher volatility. A beta of zero does not follow market moves, and a beta of less than zero implies that the stock trades in the opposite direction to the SP500.

Another criterion is the volatility, representing the price fluctuation over time. It is a negative force in an investment portfolio, because it affects the stability of the profitability and it increases the risk of loss of the principal invested. It is the standard deviation of a given security and it raises the magnitude of the variations in value of the financial asset, compared to the average performance of the sector. As such, beta is a key component of volatility.

Some alternative investments are designed not only to reduce downside risk, but also to maintain a lower level of volatility. The fund manager has to do statistical analysis to rank the values based on the expected returns and the risk factors (quantitative risk analysis), and this study helps to determine the values to choose, to increase the alpha and minimize the beta. The mathematical analysis is made based on models assisted by computers, often named "Black Box".

Many hedge funds use derivatives, which allow the manager to establish parameters for each investment, or to maximize the alpha for the fund.

Also, the APT (Arbitrage Pricing Theory) argues that the expected return on a financial investment can be modeled as a linear function of various macroeconomic factors or as hypothetical market indices, where sensitivity to variations in each factor is represented by a beta coefficient that is factor-specific. The rate of profit derived from the model is then used to estimate correctly the price of the asset - the value has to be equal to that provided at the end of the period, deducted from the rate specified by the model.

If the price diverges, the arbitration is to bring it back in line.

Ultimately, regardless of how a portfolio is to be analyzed, as long as its growth is above average, it is still the percentage of profits at the end of the year that makes a difference, as long as the volatility remains low.

In my fund, I looked at all those valuation models, but I left the task of analyzing my results to an outside agency, which, at the end of each trading day, received from my clearing house the entire position list with each trade valuation and the P&L of my portfolio. These studies were done for me according to all necessary measures so that my performance was published in accordance with the standards.

Personally, I preferred a KISS approach.

As long as I was not losing my mind with the likes of Enron or some stupid options idea, my performance was steady and I had nothing to complain about. My lessons learned had been too painful to repeat, and I enjoyed reaping the rewards of my discipline.

My use of fewer trading tools and only a couple of strategies made it easier to acquire some ease at generating regular and consistent earnings. My early and not so early errors resulted in learning and the trials and tribulations of the exercise of my profession contributed to my experience, making my work easier, even if my first few years were associated with the persistent stress to provide for the well-being of my boys.

In writing this book, my thoughts have been those of a mother, whose goal was always to teach and protect her cubs.

It is dedicated with love and affection to my sons. Every sacrifice in my life has been amply rewarded through their personal and professional success. I have particularly wanted to reveal to Maxime what I have learned throughout my career, in the hope of seeing him turn his career also into a story worth telling. I am immensely proud of him, and his brother.

I hope this book will help them understand the path I've chosen. Most importantly I want to thank them for being the source of my inspiration. During every struggle I endured and every success I achieved, I was thinking about my children and what it would mean for their future.

An even greater blessing would be to see my story prove profitable to all those who also want to embrace the career of a Wall Street trader.

To all, I sincerely wish good luck and good trading.

THE END

INDEX

ABOUT THE AUTHOR

Ninette D. Uzan-Nemitz in her quest for success became one of the first female Wall Street traders. In an industry where careers rarely last more than a couple of years, she continues to profitably invest her discipline and determination for extraordinary returns.

She has been featured in the Boston Globe, the Tokyo Shimbun and Playboy. Her story is an inspiration to all those who want to take control of their financial destiny without being eaten alive by the wolves.

Beginning in a boiler room, she struggled and succeeded, finding golden opportunities, creating a proprietary trading system and founding the Viking Hedge Fund. Along the way, she managed to avoid or escape from all the tricks and the traps of the wolves of Wall Street.

Now "retired", she trades her own accounts, lectures in leading business schools and hosts private webinars.

Ninette lives in Paris in the shadow of the Arc de Triomphe and the sunshine of her family.

www.reminiscences-trader.com

www.ingramcontent.com/pod-product-compliance
Lightning Source LLC
Chambersburg PA
CBHW072250210326
41458CB00073B/930